Raw

Raw

Recipes for a modern vegetarian lifestyle

Solla Eiríksdóttir

About the Book

It was a peaceful fall (autumn) day. My daughter Hildur and I were sitting in the family garden, washing the just-harvested carrots and beets (beetroot), enjoying the cool fall breeze, and discussing an article that we had recently read. It was about extraordinary healthy centenarians from exciting places around the world; people who have found their own way of living in harmony with their native environment, following the traditions of a long line of ancestors, and who have reaped the benefit: A long, healthy, meaningful life. Hildur and I found it fascinating and it was then that we had a realization. We have been brought up by the archetype of such long-living, healthy people. Not in some far away "exciting" place, but in our own home country, Iceland. My parents (and Hildur's grandparents) have been growing their own organic vegetables for over sixty years, living their lives in sync with the seasons, and following the rhythm of nature. This realization reminded us that sometimes we do not need to look far to find wisdom. It can be in our own backyard.

Now we are three generations, each bringing a grain of salt to the table of experience. I have a passion for raw-food cuisine, but my cooking is also influenced by living foods, macrobiotics, and traditional fermentation among other things. Hildur, studied nutritional science and brings enthusiasm and a curiosity for new information to the mix. Through our collective experience we have found our path to a healthy vegetarian lifestyle. Make homegrown or locally grown, organic whole plant foods your staple. Enjoy raw foods, some cooked foods, include fermented and living foods, and make them with a whole lot of love. That is our formula.

In this book we wish to share with you our passion for delicious, nutritious food and our fascination for the enchanting cycle of the seasons. We have included healthy recipes to take you right through the day, from morning to evening, as well as delicious sweet treats. We have also included special seasonal recipes and activities, which we feel help to connect us to the rhythm of life. Our hope is to inspire readers, wherever they are, to find their unique way to lead healthy, meaningful lives in the modern world.

Introduction

Like Mother Like Daughter

We made the transition from being a mother and daughter to being a grandmother and mother when Hildur had her first child a few years ago. We began to spend more time together through taking care of the new family member. By spending more time with the family, we have made more time for cooking, gardening, and learning about new inspiring things, such as the natural dyeing of fabrics and upcycling. Some of our shared goals in life are to inspire as many people as possible to lead a healthy lifestyle, eat more vegetables and raw foods, and to be kind to one another, especially Mother Earth.

Solla

When I was growing up, the selection of fruits and vegetables in Icelandic stores was sparse and very dependant upon the seasons. You could find fresh potatoes, turnips, kale, apples, and oranges and that's about it. A common meal was boiled fish and potatoes, or meat soup with turnips and potatoes, but due to globalization, it has now changed considerably over the past few decades. Historically, Icelanders were not the biggest vegetable consumers, mostly because of the weather and growing conditions.

The food was a little different in my childhood home. My parents have always lived in Reykjavík but they started growing organic vegetables in a garden just outside the city and they still do so sixty years later. My three brothers and I grew up helping out in the garden in spring and summer, harvesting in fall (autumn), and enjoying eating different vegetables throughout a large part of the year. I have many fond memories and remember vividly one late summer's day when we were out in the garden and all of a sudden I was starving. I asked my mother for something to eat and she suggested that I pick anything I liked from the garden. I pulled up a whole bucket of small but flavorful carrots and in that moment I had an epiphany: From now on I only wanted to eat food straight from the ground. Of course this was not possible, but this feeling is something that has always stayed with me, and newly picked vegetables will always be my favorite.

In the summer, fall (autumn), and early winter, we always had plenty of fresh vegetables, and my parents developed storage methods so that the harvest could last until next spring. My parents were teachers, and growing vegetables was not a traditional way to spend their spare time. When I look back they might not have been the most mainstream people around. My mother had decided to become a vegetarian at the age of thirteen, which was highly unusual. However, we didn't follow a strict vegetarian diet when I was growing up because it was difficult to get a variety of vegetables during the winter. My father did most of the cooking, which he learned from his mother, who stayed with the Seventh Day Adventists in Copenhagen for a while in her youth and was influenced by their lifestyle and vegetarian diet. Later I learned that she had also been inspired by a book she read back in the 1950s: *The Miracle of Living Foods* by Dr. Kristine Nolfi. I am very grateful for what I learned from my parents and I have been building on it ever since.

I was only nineteen when Hildur was born, and for her first few years we lived in Denmark. Even though I had been brought up with homegrown vegetables and loving parents who cooked nourishing foods, I had never been expected to help out in the kitchen, so I didn't know how to cook anything. My first meal as a housewife was a disaster. I served burned ground (minced) meat with remoulade and very undercooked potatoes. I didn't think much of it and thought I just had to accept that my talents lay elsewhere and we would have to live with my primitive way of cooking. But my life took a U-turn one day when I went to see the doctor. I had suffered from allergies from childhood and they had been getting worse, so I went to a doctor in Copenhagen to see if he could give me an allergy injection. Hildur was three months old at the time, so I took her with me. As I was speaking with the doctor she started crying and to console her I breastfed her. The doctor quickly told me that I would have to stop breastfeeding altogether after receiving the injection. This was quite a shock, so I decided that I had to think about it before going ahead with the injection and went out for a walk. I was really desperate because I did not want to give up breastfeeding, but I also felt terrible because of my allergies. As I was wandering around, feeling totally hopeless, I stumbled upon a health food store in a small basement. I went inside and there I met an herbalist that would soon change my life forever. I told him about my worries and he said that he and his wife would like to try to help me. I signed up for a cooking class and they taught me how to cook. I cut out sugar and refined foods from my diet and learned how to use all these "exotic" ingredients. In the following years I studied yoga, macrobiotic cooking, and meditation and never returned to the doctor, because my allergies slowly got better and finally disappeared. I don't know the scientific explanation for this, but it was a huge turning point—my outlook had changed for life, and I also learned how to cook.

When we moved back to Iceland, we lived with my parents for many years, and so Hildur was also brought up helping out in my parents' organic garden. I studied visual arts and textiles, but my passion for healthy vegetarian food had grown strong and I started cooking for a living. I finally started my own vegetarian restaurant in the nineties. In 1996 I heard about raw living foods through a friend. I was intrigued and bought the next ticket out to Puerto Rico to learn about living foods at Ann Wigmor's center. Dr. Ann Wigmore (1909–1994) was a Lithuanian-American health practitioner, nutritionist, whole food advocate, and author. She was a pioneer in the use of wheatgrass juice and raw and living foods for detoxifying and healing the body. The concept of living foods is in some ways different from the new raw food methods that are popular now. Dr. Ann put a special focus on making every meal highly nutritious and easily digestible with methods such as soaking, sprouting, fermentation, and blending. She believed that by using these methods the foods would be relieved from their dormant state or hibernation (seeds and grains waiting for the right conditions to "wake up") and become active and alive. As such, they are easier on the digestion and the nutrients can be absorbed more easily. My younger daughter Júlía, then four years old, traveled with me and I learned how to make energy soup, rejuvelac, sprouts, seed milk, nut cheese, to grow indoor greens, and a lot more. I loved this new way of preparing foods and have adopted many of them to my lifestyle back home in Iceland. Since then I have been using raw food methods as one of the numerous ways to prepare delicious food, adding variety, and new inspirations to my kitchen.

Today, my cooking is influenced by everything I have learned over the years. I don't adhere to one particular diet or food philosophy, other than using a lot of fresh vegetables, preferably organic, and sustainably grown foods, and my secret ingredient in every recipe is a whole lot of love.

Hildur

I was raised on mostly plant foods, although at the time I wasn't really aware of the fact that I was a vegetarian. The term was not so common in those days. I later realized that when people talked about home food my understanding of the term was quite different from theirs. Of course, I gradually became aware that the food at my friends' houses was different from what I was used to, but it took a while to realize that we were a little bit "special" in other people's view. At the time I wasn't particularly interested in food other than it being a necessary fuel, so I didn't think much about it. My grandparents grew vegetables and my grandmother fermented a large part of the harvest to keep for winter, so we had fermented carrots and beets (beetroots) with every meal. My mother was always very adventurous in the kitchen, and from time to time she would turn the kitchen into a greenhouse full of wheatgrass and greens of all possible kinds. There were jars packed with sprouts, rejuvelac, almond cheese in the making, tofu-making projects in the basement, and so on. My lunch was usually miso soup with seaweeds and a green and purple energy soup, which my friends found very dubious to say the least. But in my eyes, their food was just as exotic. Times have certainly changed and today my family's approach to food is not unusual.

From an early age I was focused on becoming a professional musician, and as a teen and young adult I was blessed to be able to travel a lot through my music. One of my favorite things about traveling was to try out new vegetarian foods and discover different books on food and cooking. In my spare time, I usually found myself in a bookstore pouring over books on how to make exotic vegetarian foods. I loved to read and buy books on how to make your own tofu from scratch, the wonders of fermentation, how to grow "superfoods" in your kitchen, how to dye fabrics with something from the garden, and how to upcycle old clothes. One day I realized that every obscure book I had brought home from places around the world was always something my mother or grandmother had already been experimenting with while I was growing up. This was a big revelation for me. I thought I was bringing home exciting news from the other side of the world but the knowledge was in my own backyard the whole time. At this time I was also studying nutritional science and found it remarkable to see how my family's lifestyle fitted in exactly with what all the experts were advising. I started regaining interest in my roots and family traditions. I became eager to learn all I possibly could from my grandparents and mother. I asked my grandfather to help me set up my own composting system. I asked my grandmother to teach me how to ferment vegetables and advise me on my vegetable garden, and I asked my mother to teach me how to master exciting vegetarian dishes. There is something so deeply fascinating about wisdom and skills that have accumulated through the generations. In the past decade there has been a noticeable rise in the interest in kitchen crafts from the past. Homegrown vegetables, fermenting, sourdough, and home-cooked meals in general are gaining in popularity. I have a feeling that our traditional family recipes will be relevant to many people across the world.

A Diet High in Raw Foods

When we choose homegrown or local, organic, seasonal, and raw foods we receive our food in the state where it has its highest nutritional value. Transport, storage, and cooking each take a toll and result in a decrease in nutrients. Most plant foods are naturally rich in fibre, vitamins, minerals, antioxidants, phytonutrients, and enzymes. Some of these compounds are sensitive to heat and a significant amount can be lost in the process of cooking. Enzymes denature at a temperature around 118°F/48°C and so many raw food enthusiasts believe that it is best to prepare a large proportion of their food below this temperature. Enzymes are proteins that catalyze digestion and the raw food theory says that if food contains enough enzymes it will be easier to digest. Thus the body can spend its energy and resources on repairing and healing instead of using too much on digestion.

The raw food lifestyle has many followers. Some like to eliminate all foods heated above 118°F/48°C, while others feel better eating 80 percent raw, 20 percent cooked. A diet containing more than 50 percent raw plant food is considered a high-raw diet. Many people feel that it is an easier diet to maintain than one that's 100 percent raw.

Hildur and I live in Iceland—a cold climate—and so it can be difficult to maintain a diet that's 100 percent raw. We like to listen to our bodies and we find that we feel best on a high-raw diet, with a mix of living foods for efficient digestion but also some warm cooked foods, especially in the winter. In the cold season, we find that fermented foods and sprouts give us great energy when combined with a mix of cooked and raw foods. In the summer, however, we often feel like eating a bigger proportion of raw foods. This way we reap the benefits from eating a high proportion of raw foods without eliminating cooked foods.

When making dietary changes, it is always a good idea to do a gradual change, letting the body (and mind) adjust at a rate that suits you. Every individual is different and it is key to listen to the signals your body is sending.

We recommend that you focus on gradually adding more nutritious plant foods to your diet, and in time there will be little space left for the foods that do not make you feel good. Instead of focusing on what to eliminate, we like to focus on what goodness to add. It can be good to start with changing your breakfast and then gradually add healthy meals to the rest of your day at your own pace.

Please make an appointment to see your doctor before starting a new diet plan, especially if you have underlying medical conditions or are pregnant.

Plant-Based Whole Foods

We can reap many health benefits by eating more plant foods. Healthy plant-based diets are rich in vegetables, fruit, beans, legumes (pulses), whole grains, nuts, seeds, and spices. And they are highly nutritious, because they contain plenty of fiber, vitamins, minerals, antioxidants, and phytonutrients. Most experts on nutrition agree that eating more vegetables is an essential part of leading a healthy lifestyle. Plant-based diets also play a big role in reducing greenhouse gas emissions, and by reducing consumption of animal products, we can help the environment in many ways. According to reports from The Food and Agriculture Organization of the United Nations, the livestock industry produces more greenhouse gasses each year than global transport, and uses too much water to be sustainable. Growing demand for meat and dairy is thus of great concern for our planet. A plant-based diet uses up less energy and resources than a diet heavy on animal products and is therefore more sustainable. Not everyone wants to become a vegetarian, but every effort counts and we can all benefit from eating more good-quality plant-based whole foods.

We have found that many people are intimidated by ingredients that they are unfamiliar with, so one of our goals in life is to demystify such ingredients and teach as many people as possible how to prepare delicious home-cooked meals, bursting with flavors, using good-quality whole food ingredients and sensible cooking methods. Be careful not to use more heat than necessary or to deep fry, and be careful of heating oils too much (it's better to add good-quality oils to meals after cooking). A lot of nutrients are heat sensitive: Some will disappear with too much heat; others, such as good-quality oils, will turn bad and become unhealthy. This is part of the reason why a high-raw, part living foods diet (see page 13) is beneficial. It doesn't have to be complicated. Let your imagination loose, take your taste buds on an adventurous journey, and be inspired.

When we make time to prepare meals from scratch, we have more control over what ingredients we use and avoid highly processed and refined foods. Eating healthily is about more than just quality foods and getting an adequate amount of nutrients; it is about taking time to enjoy the moment, enjoy the meal, and to spend more time with the people we love and friends who enrich our lives. Our mindset is very important, and when we make the effort to enjoy and notice the food we are eating we will probably feel more satisfied after it. It is important to listen to the signals our bodies are sending to us, because they are incredibly good at giving us clues and letting us know which foods make us feel good and how much we actually need to eat. Sometimes we eat fast, convenient food or candies (sweets) just out of habit without actually being hungry or needing them, but we can train ourselves to become much better at noticing what we really want and need, and observing whether we are actually hungry or full. Let's make time to enjoy our food and eat with a conscious mind. In our experience, it is best to take small steps and focus on what delicious healthy foods we can add to our diet gradually, instead of eliminating everything "bad" all at once. If you find yourself eating foods that make you feel guilty, don't worry, just enjoy the moment. Changing your eating habits over time will happen, for sure, but the important thing is to let exceptions be enjoyable—it's what we eat most of the time that really counts.

An Organic and Eco-Friendly Lifestyle

We feel that we should be doing everything in our power to take good care of Mother Nature, so she can continue to take care of us. Growing up in a home where organic vegetables were a staple, we understand that it is possible to grow food in harmony with the environment.

In organic agriculture, synthetic chemical fertilizers and pesticides, hormones, and antibiotics are not used. Methods such as crop rotation and compost are used to maintain a healthy soil, which is the foundation for a healthy crop. The goal is to sustain ecological balance, enhance biodiversity, and promote sustainability.

An organic way of growing is going back to our roots, to a time before we were dependant upon chemical pesticides and fertilizers. It was only in the twentieth century that these chemicals were introduced in such large quantities, so in a sense organic farming could be viewed as the traditional method instead of being the other way around. By supporting organic agriculture, we can help change people's perception of organic foods as something traditional and normal again, rather than as a luxury. This is important, not only for our planet but also for our health, and most importantly for our children's and our grandchildren's future. We do not know how long-term accumulation of pesticide residues will affect us, and we believe that the soil, the water, and the whole eco system should be nourished in the most natural and sustainable ways possible.

Through growing our own food we learn to view nature and her gifts in a different way. We begin to understand how valuable good soil is, how each and every plant is precious, and we feel heartbroken when we see food thrown away. Food scraps are valuable because they can be turned into nourishing soil, which in the circle of life, keeps giving.

We can do our part in protecting our environment by starting with small changes in our own lives. Grandpa Eiríkur and Grandma Hildur have taught us so much about life through their beautiful lifestyle—to take good care of ourselves and others, our precious planet, and also our material possessions. When we take care of the items we own, we don't have to buy new things all the time—we can reuse and upcycle them and recycle items that can't be reused. We don't have to be perfect but each gesture counts. Everyone can make small changes in the right direction but the change starts with us.

The Seasons

The seasons play a big role in every Icelander's life. The geographical placement of the island means that every single day of the year is different in terms of sunlight and length of the day. On the longest days of summer, around the Summer Solstice, the sun rises at 3 a.m. and sets around midnight. This means that the sun is up for twenty-one hours. But on the shortest winter days we only get four hours of daylight. In some narrow fjords in the western and eastern part of Iceland, the surrounding mountains are so high that the sun doesn't reach over for weeks or even months. The inhabitants have a tradition to celebrate the day when they finally see the sun again with *Sólarkaffi* (sun coffee) and pancakes for everyone.

These extremes and the whole scale in between makes our activities, traditions, and even our moods very connected to the seasons. For this reason, in addition to chapters of recipes, which will take you through the day from morning to evening, we have included a few seasonal recipes and projects in this book, where you can feel the atmosphere of each unique season.

In the darkest period of winter, many people feel like sleeping longer and crave comforting warm foods. Skiing is a popular pastime but we also spend a lot of time inside our warm houses. We love to bake a healthier version of Chocolate Cookies (see page 198), but also find it very rewarding to grow some indoor greens (see pages 193–4), while the flora outside sleeps under a white blanket of snow.

When the days get longer and the sun climbs higher in the sky, it is almost as though we are waking up from a long period of hibernation. We can feel the general mood of everyone lift—huge smiles and happy faces everywhere. We have been craving brighter days and are ready to go outside. In the spring everything comes to life again and we can start growing vegetables and greens, even if it's only on a sunny windowsill or outside on a balcony. We include instructions for growing vegetables in small spaces (see pages 59–60) because we believe that everyone can grow something, no matter the size of home. Rhubarb grows in many gardens and is among the first crops of the season—oh how lovely is the scent of Rhubarb Jam (see page 64) bubbling away on the stove.

In the summer, we enjoy ice pops (ice lollies, see pages 111–2) in shorts and summer dresses even though the thermometer only says 50°F (10°C); we are so determined to enjoy the sun. Life is all about picnics (see page 113–9), bike rides, barbecues, and other outdoor activities. At this time of year, we love to dye cloth with natural colors from the kitchen and hang it up to dry in the sun (see page 104). We get a lot of energy from the sunlight and many people need less sleep in the summer. It is easy to wake up when the sun is already shining and an adventurous day awaits outside.

Fall (autumn) is our personal favourite. It's harvest time. Whether we grow our own vegetables or are thankful for someone else making the effort, we can buy plenty of fresh vegetables in the stores. This is a joyful time when everything is brimming with fresh produce. Icelanders go out and pick wild berries that grow on the hillsides. It is a very common household activity to make wild berry jams and pies (see pages 153–4) at this time of year, and of course, we like to prepare for the winter by fermenting vegetables (see pages 155–7) and storing fresh herbs (see page 158). The fascinating circle of life and seasons keeps on moving.

The Recipes and Special Diets

All the recipes are vegetarian and are labeled dairy free, gluten free, nut free, raw food, and vegan (see symbols below), where relevant, to help those people with allergies or following a specific diet to see which recipes are suitable for them. A vegan diet consists solely of plant foods. All animal products, such as eggs, cheese and other dairy, and honey are avoided. All of the recipes are wheat free and most are naturally gluten free and vegan. If you have a nut allergy, it can be possible to substitute nuts and almonds with seeds, shredded coconut, or pine nuts. We have not listed these options everywhere, but it should be easy to do. If you are strict about eating raw foods, make sure to use raw cacao, raw nut butters, and so on. If you are not following a strict raw-food diet then you can enjoy making the raw-inspired desserts using ingredients such as semisweet (plain) chocolate and unsweetened cocoa powder—they will taste absolutely delicious.

Now, let's not waste any more time—dive in and let the fun begin.

(DF) Dairy Free

(GF) Gluten Free

NF Nut Free*

R Raw Food

V Vegan

*Some nut-free recipes may include coconut, coconut products, and/ or pine nuts.

Morning

Breakfast

First Bite

—

Spring Recipes and Activities

Eating well in the morning sets you up for a great day. Because every person is an individual, Hildur and I think it is important to learn to trust what our body is trying to tell us in terms of what is best for us. So what gives you the best energy and focus for the day? Some people feel good when they skip breakfast or have a very light meal, while others swear by a big hearty meal that keeps them feeling full until lunch. In this chapter there are a variety of options for breakfast and, hopefully, everyone can find something to their liking. It is usual to have food that's on the sweeter side in the morning, such as sweet cereal and sugary yogurt but we have tried our best to steer away from refined sugars at this time of the day and instead focus on incorporating healthy greens, vegetables, nuts, seeds, whole grains, and fruit into our meals.

One thing we have found that makes a good morning turn into an even better day is to have a positive mindset. Some people achieve this by starting their morning with meditation. We love listening to music that sparks warm, inspiring feelings and we believe that it can help start the day in a positive way, especially when the music is something that brings up good memories and enjoyable moments. Why not even sing along to it and dance while making breakfast? Then you can walk out and embrace the day with a positive feeling.

Homemade Energy Mix

Makes 3 tablespoons

- 1 tablespoon hemp seeds
- 1 teaspoon ashwagandha
- 1 teaspoon moringa powder
- 1 teaspoon ground turmeric
- 1 teaspoon lucuma powder
- 1 teaspoon bee pollen
- ½ teaspoon maca powder

This mixture of "superfoods" can be kept in an airtight jar for a few weeks. We like to add 1 teaspoon of this energy mix to our basic morning smoothie (see below).

Put all the ingredients into a sterilized glass jar and mix together. The energy mix can be stored for up to 2 months. You can add it to your morning smoothie or just simply mix it into a glass of water or coconut water and drink. The perfect amount to use for each smoothie is 1 teaspoon.

Tip: To sterilize jars and lids, wash them in hot soapy water, rinse, and dry in an oven preheated to 250°F/120°C/Gas Mark ½. Alternatively, put them into a dishwasher and make sure they are dry before using.

Green Morning Smoothie

Serves 2

- 2 cups (16 fl oz/475 ml) water or coconut water
- 1 ripe avocado, peeled, pitted, and cubed
- 2 cups (7 oz/200 g) cucumber chunks
- 1 lime, quartered
- ½ cup (1 oz/25 g) or 1 handful chopped cilantro (coriander)
- 1 tablespoon hemp seeds
- 3 inch/7.5 cm (about 2¼ oz/60 g) piece of fresh ginger root, peeled and quartered
- 2 inch/5 cm (about 1 oz/25 g) piece of fresh turmeric root, peeled and quartered
- 1–2 teaspoons Homemade Energy Mix (see above)
- 2–3 drops of peppermint oil (optional)
- 2 oz/50 g or 1 handful spinach, kale, or green leaf lettuce
- a few ice cubes

If you prefer your smoothie sweeter, then add some fruit to the blend. Blueberries, raspberries, mango, apples, and pitted dates are all good.

Put all the ingredients into a blender and blend until smooth. Pour into glasses and serve.

Turmeric Smoothie/Shake

Serves 2

- ¼ cup (1 oz/30 g) hemp seeds
- 1 cup (5 oz/150 g) frozen mango chunks
- ½ banana
- 1 tablespoon coconut oil
- 2 teaspoons shredded ginger root
- 2 teaspoons lemon juice
- 1 teaspoon chia seeds
- ½–¾ teaspoon turmeric (use either ground fresh root or powder)
- ½ teaspoon ground cardamom powder

Hemp seed milk is a quick milk to make. Unlike almond milk, wich requires the nuts to be soaked, you don't have to soak the seeds. Use 1 part hemp seeds to 3–4 parts water.

Put the hemp seeds and ¾ cup (6 fl oz/175 ml) water into a blender and blend until you have your hemp seed milk.

Add the remaining ingredients to the blender and blend until smooth. Pour into glasses and serve.

Morning Boost

Serves 2

- ½ cup (2¾ oz/75 g) almonds
- 1½ cups (8 oz/225 g) frozen blueberries
- ½–1 banana, cut into chunks
- ½ avocado, peeled and cubed
- 1 tablespoon raw chia seeds
- 1 handful of spinach
- 1 tablespoon flaxseed oil
- 2 capsules of probiotic or acidophilus supplements (optional)
- Homemade Energy Mix, to serve (see page 22)

Soak the almonds in a bowl of cold water for 8 hours, or overnight.

The next day, drain the almonds and pat them dry on paper towels. Discard the water. Put the almonds and 1½ cups (12 fl oz/350 ml) water into a blender and blend until you have your delicious almond milk. Add the remaining ingredients and blend until smooth. If you are using probiotics, then add at the end and blend briefly on slow speed to make sure they are mixed in.

You can pour the morning boost just as it comes into glasses for children and then add 1 teaspoon of the energy mix to the blend for grown-ups.

Homemade Nut Milk
A Tutorial

Makes generous 2 cups
(17 fl oz/500 ml) milk

- 1 cup (5 oz/150 g) nuts or seeds
- sweetener, of your choice (optional)
- spices of your choice, such as cinnamon, vanilla, and cardamom (optional)

Homemade nut milk is easier to make than you may think. Hildur and I make nut milk a couple of times every week, so we always have some ready in the refrigerator.

When you make your own milk, you are able to control the consistency, and more importantly, use a sweetener of your choice, or even choose not to sweeten it. We like to presoak the nuts or seeds because it makes the milk easier to digest and more of the nutrients will be absorbed into the body. To achieve a smooth consistency, we strain the milk through a nut milk bag (see page 233), and then use the pulp (nut/almond meal) that's left behind in the bag for baking. If you don't have a nut milk bag then strain the milk through a piece of cheesecloth (muslin) placed over a bowl.

Put the nuts or seeds of your choice into a bowl, pour in enough water to cover, and then soak for 8 hours.

Drain the nuts or seeds in a strainer (sieve) and rinse under cold running water. Put the nuts or seeds into a blender with scant 2 cups (15 fl oz/ 450 ml) fresh water and blend well. If you prefer a smooth milk, then pour the mixture through a nut milk bag or a piece of cheesecloth (muslin) set over a bowl.

Next, sweeten the milk with a sweetener and spices of your choice, if desired, then pour the milk into a clean, sterilized glass bottle (see page 22) and seal with a lid. The milk can be stored in the refrigerator for a few days.

Tips: You can use almond butter or sesame seed paste (tahini) instead of the nuts or seeds, if you prefer. Freeze the nut or seed pulp if you are not using it soon.

Chia and Millet Flake Porridge

Serves 2

- 1 cup (8 fl oz/250 ml) almond milk (page 26)
- 3 tablespoons chia seeds
- 1 cup (3½ oz/100 g) rolled millet flakes
- 1 teaspoon vanilla powder
- 1 teaspoon ground cinnamon
- ½ teaspoon lemon juice
- a pinch of salt
- ½ banana, thinly sliced, for topping

For the raspberry compote
- 1 pear, peeled, cored, and chopped into small pieces or grated
- 1 cup (4½ oz/130 g) raspberries (fresh or frozen)
- 1 tablespoon shredded fresh ginger root

If you don't have much time in the mornings, then this method of making porridge (oatmeal) is great. It is easy to make the night before and can also be made several days ahead. Just be careful to store the compote and porridge in separate containers and assemble it the same day as serving.

Put the almond milk and chia seeds into a clean glass jar, put the lid on, and shake for 2–3 minutes, or until combined. Stir in the millet flakes, vanilla, cinnamon, lemon juice, and salt, then put the lid back on and set aside to rest for 15–30 minutes, or overnight.

For the compote, put the pear, raspberries, and ginger into a medium bowl and mash with a fork until it is the consistency you like. We like it slightly chunky. Alternatively, place the ingredients into a food processor and process using the pulse button.

When ready to serve, pour half the raspberry compote into a bowl or a glass jar, add the chia porridge (oatmeal), and top with a layer of thinly sliced banana. Spoon the remaining raspberry compote on top and eat.

Red Shot

Serves 1

- scant ½ cup (1 oz/30 g) goji berries
- seeds from 1 pomegranate
- scant ½ cup (3½ fl oz/100 ml) beet (beetroot) juice
- 1 small red chile, seeded
- 1 teaspoon acai powder

A shot is more concentrated than a smoothie and has little fiber, which means the nutrients enter your system faster and you get a hit of energy.

Put the goji berries into a bowl, pour in enough water to cover, and soak for 30 minutes, then drain.

Put the soaked goji berries into a blender with the remaining ingredients and blend well. Strain through a nut milk bag or a piece of cheesecloth (muslin) set over a bowl, then pour into a glass and it's ready to drink.

Yellow Shot

Serves 1

- 2 inch (5 cm) piece of fresh ginger root, peeled
- 2 tablespoons water or coconut water
- 1 teaspoon lemon juice
- ½ teaspoon apple cider vinegar
- ¼ teaspoon ground turmeric
- ⅛ teaspoon black pepper

Use a microplane, zester, or grater to grate the ginger finely and then squeeze the paste in your hands over a bowl to catch the juice. (You will be surprised by how much juice will come out.) You need 1 teaspoon of pressed ginger.

Put the pressed ginger into a clean jar with the remaining ingredients, put the lid on, and shake together. It's ready to drink.

Pink Shot

Serves 1

- 1 blood grapefruit, peeled
- 1 lime, peeled
- 2 inch (5 cm) piece of fresh ginger root, peeled

Put the fruit and ginger through a juicer or blend well in a blender. Strain the liquid through a nut milk bag or a piece of cheesecloth (muslin) set over a bowl, then pour into a glass and it's ready to drink.

Green Shot

Serves 1

- 2 limes, peeled
- 2 kaffir lime leaves
- ¾ inch (2 cm) piece of fresh ginger root, peeled
- 1 teaspoon wheatgrass powder

Put all the ingredients into a blender and blend well. Strain through a nut milk bag or a piece of cheesecloth (muslin) set over a bowl, then pour into a glass and it's ready to drink.

Chocolate Chia Pudding with Granola and Fruit

Serves 2–3

- ¼ cup (1½ oz/40 g) chia seeds
- 1 cup (8 fl oz/250 ml) almond milk
- 2 tablespoons raw cacao powder
- 2 teaspoons coconut nectar, maple syrup, or another sweetener of your choice, to taste
- 1 teaspoon vanilla powder
- 1 cup (4 oz/120 g) Homemade Granola (see page 38)
- 1½ cups (7½ oz/215 g) fresh, seasonal berries

Chia seeds are an all-time favorite and are perfect for making into breakfast puddings. The texture is great, but they are also nutritious, and they are incredibly rich in fiber, and therefore filling. Chia seeds can be soaked ahead of time. When soaked in just water, they can be kept for a few weeks in the refrigerator, but if you add almond milk or spices only keep them for a few days before using.

Put the chia seeds, almond milk, cacao powder, sweetener, and vanilla powder in a clean glass jar. Put the lid on and shake for 1–2 minutes, or until the mixture has blended well together. Let stand in the refrigerator for 1 hour, or overnight. The seeds will expand and have a jellylike consistency.

When ready to serve, spoon a layer of the chia pudding into the bottom of 2–3 glasses, add a layer of the granola, then add a layer of berries on top. Repeat the layers until everything has been used.

Homemade Brazil Nut and Cashew Yogurt

Serves 2

- 1½ cups (8 oz/225 g) cashew nuts
- 1 teaspoon chia seeds, ground in a clean coffee or spice grinder
- 1 teaspoon probiotic powder
- 1½ tablespoons lemon juice
- pumpkin seeds, fresh berries, or fruit, to serve

For the Brazil nut milk
- ⅔ cup (3½ oz/100 g) Brazil nuts

This delicious yogurt recipe was our favorite before the selection of plant-based yogurts available in the grocery stores became as good as it is today. However, it is still very rewarding to make and the distinct yogurty flavor comes as a pleasant surprise every time.

Put the cashew nuts into a bowl, pour in enough water to cover, and soak for at least 2 hours, or overnight. Drain, rinse under cold running water, and set aside. Discard the soaking water.

To make the Brazil nut milk, put the Brazil nuts into a bowl, pour in enough water to cover, and soak for 2 hours. Drain, rinse under cold running water, and put into a blender. Pour in 1¼ cups (10 fl oz/300 ml) fresh water and blend well. Strain the mixture through a nut milk bag or a piece of cheesecloth (muslin) set over a bowl. Pour into a sterilized (see page 22) bottle and set aside. You will need 1¼ cups (10 fl oz/300 ml) for this recipe.

Pour 1¼ cups (10 fl oz/300 ml) of the Brazil nut milk into a blender, add the ground chia seeds, probiotic powder, and lemon juice and blend together well. Pour the mixture into a sterilized glass jar and cover the mouth of the jar with a clean dish cloth. Wrap a rubber band around the cloth so it stays in place and let stand in a warm place for 12 hours. The following morning you will smell the sweet yogurt scent arising from the jar.

Put the yogurt in a blender with the soaked cashews and blend until smooth. The yogurt is ready to be served and enjoyed. It can be kept in an airtight container in the refrigerator for a few days. Serve sprinkled with pumpkin seeds, fresh berries, or fruit.

Homemade Granola

Makes 8 cups (2 lb/900 g)

For the granola
- 3 cups (9 oz/255 g) rolled oats
- 2 cups (5 oz/150 g) shredded coconut
- 1 cup (5 oz/150 g) chopped almonds
- ½ cup (2 oz/50 g) pumpkin seeds
- ½ cup (2½ oz/75 g) sunflower seeds
- 2 tablespoons sesame seeds
- 2 tablespoons chia seeds
- 2 tablespoons hemp seeds
- 2 tablespoons flaxseeds

For the sauce
- 2 bags favorite chai tea
- 2 tablespoons sweetener, such as coconut palm sugar, maple syrup, or Date Paste (see page 202), optional
- ¼ cup (1¼ oz/35 g) sesame seed paste (tahini)
- 2 tablespoons coconut oil

We both love granola. Often granolas are loaded with sugar and so we like to make our own from scratch because we can control how sweet it is and also use all our favorite ingredients. A great trick when you want to cut down on sweeteners is to use chai tea for a delicious sweet and spicy taste. For this recipe, we love to use gluten-free oats but you can use ordinary rolled oats too. If you are nut free or have a nut allergy, then use more sunflower and pumpkin seeds instead of the almonds.

Preheat the oven to 350°F/180°C/Gas Mark 4.

To make the sauce, pour ½ cup (4 fl oz/120 ml) water into a bowl, add the tea bags, and let soak for 5 minutes. Remove and discard the tea bags and pour the tea into a blender. Add the remaining ingredients and blend until smooth. Set aside.

For the granola, put all the ingredients into a large bowl and mix together. Pour in the sauce and stir together until all the ingredients are coated in the sauce.

Put a baking sheet on an oven tray. Spread the granola mixture onto the sheet and bake for 30–40 minutes, stirring every 10 minutes so it bakes evenly and does not burn.

Green Energy Soup with Acai, Pears, and Seaweed

Serves 2

- ½ cup (4 fl oz/120 ml) coconut water
- 2 kale leaves or a handful of spinach
- ½ zucchini (courgette), cut into chunks
- ½ pear, peeled, cored, and cut into chunks
- ½ avocado, peeled and cut into chunks
- ¼ cucumber, cut into chunks
- 1 handful of alfalfa sprouts
- 2 dates (optional)
- 1 tablespoon lemon juice
- 4 inch (10 cm) piece dulse, finely chopped
- a small piece of fresh chile
- 2–3 drops of edible essential oil to add some flavor (optional)

To garnish
- 1 teaspoon acai berry powder
- 2 tablespoons fresh berries of your choice

Dr. Ann Wigmore (1909–1994) was a Lithuanian-American health practitioner, nutritionist, whole-food advocate, and author. She was a pioneer in the use of wheatgrass juice as well as raw and living foods for detoxifying and healing the body. She was famous for her energy soup and this is one of the recipes that I learned to make in Puerto Rico in the nineties. It has been a part of our diet ever since because it makes us feel so good. When drinking smoothies or eating an energy soup we always chew on the first few sips to help start our digestive system working. Chewing stimulates enzyme production and helps the body to get ready for digesting food. This is our version of the famous energy soup.

Put all the ingredients into a blender and blend until smooth. Pour the soup into serving bowls, sprinkle with the acai berry powder and fresh berries and serve.

Tip: If you like, you can also garnish with ½ a pear. Peel, core, and cut the pear into pieces. Sprinkle it on with the berries and serve.

Tofu Scramble with Kale and Avocado

Serves 2–3

- 2 tablespoons olive oil
- ¼ onion, finely chopped
- 2 cloves garlic, chopped
- 4 kale leaves, stems (stalks) removed

For the tofu marinade
- 2–3 tablespoons almond milk
- 2 tablespoons nutritional yeast flakes
- 1 tablespoons tamari
- 1 tablespoon mustard
- ½ teaspoon ground turmeric
- ¼ teaspoon red pepper (chili) flakes
- a pinch of salt
- 1 cup (9 oz/250 g) tofu

To garnish
- ½ avocado, sliced
- sprouts of your choice (optional)

Start by marinating the tofu. Stir the almond milk, nutritional yeast flakes, tamari, mustard, turmeric, red pepper (chili) flakes, and salt together in a bowl. Before adding the tofu, squeeze out all the liquid. A good way to do this is to wrap the tofu in a clean dish cloth and squeeze it gently so the water comes out through the cloth. Be gentle so the tofu doesn't become a paste. You may need to use 2 cloths because a lot of liquid is likely to come out. When all of the water has been squeezed out, crumble the tofu into a bowl with all the remaining marinade ingredients, and mix to combine.

Heat the olive oil in a saucepan over medium heat. Add the onion and garlic and cook for 3–4 minutes, or until golden brown. Add the kale leaves, stir for 1 minute, then add the tofu and cook for another 4–5 minutes. Serve in a bowl and garnish with sliced avocado and sprouts, if using.

Savory Morning Bowl

Serves 2

- ½ cup (2½ oz/75 g) quinoa
- 2 inch/5 cm piece of fresh ginger root, peeled
- a pinch of sea salt flakes
- a pinch of red pepper (chili) flakes
- 1–2 teaspoons toasted sesame oil
- 4 kale leaves, stems (stalks) removed and leaves chopped
- 1 avocado, peeled, pitted, and cut into cubes
- ⅓ cup (2 oz/50 g) pistachios, toasted

For the raita
- ½ cup (2½ oz/75 g) cashew nuts
- ½ cucumber
- 1 clove garlic
- 2 dates, pitted
- 2 teaspoons nutritional yeast flakes
- 1 teaspoon onion powder
- 2 tablespoons lemon juice
- ½ teaspoon sea salt
- freshly ground black pepper

To garnish
- 2–4 sprigs cilantro (coriander)
- cress, to sprinkle
- 1 lime, cut into wedges

In the mornings we sometimes automatically go for sweet food, such as flavoring porridge (oatmeal) with dried or fresh fruit. However, this bowl is different. It is one of our favorites when we don't feel like having a sweet breakfast, but want something savory and nourishing as our first meal. Try it, it's delicious.

Put the cashew nuts for the raita into a bowl, pour in enough cold water to cover, and soak for at least 2 hours. Drain and set aside.

Put the quinoa into a saucepan with 1 cup (8 fl oz/ 250 ml) water, the ginger, sea salt, and red pepper (chili) flakes. Bring to a boil and boil for 15 minutes. All the water should be absorbed.

Meanwhile, heat the toasted sesame oil in a separate saucepan over medium heat. Add the kale and cook for about 2 minutes, or until crisp. Set aside.

For the raita, coarsely grate the cucumber and squeeze out all the excess liquid. Set aside.

Put the cashew nuts, garlic, dates, nutritional yeast flakes, onion powder, lemon juice, and ½ cup (4 fl oz/120 ml) water into a blender and blend until smooth. Season to taste with salt and pepper. Transfer to a bowl, add the cucumber, and stir together to combine. Chill in the refrigerator until ready to serve.

When the quinoa is cooked, place it in a bowl with the kale, avocado, and toasted pistachios. Garnish with the cilantro (coriander), cress, and lime wedges and serve with the raita on the side.

Chaga Latte

Serves 2

- ⅓ cup (2 oz/50 g) cashew nuts
- 1¼ cups (10 fl oz/300 ml) hot cinnamon and licorice tea made with an organic store-bought tea bag
- 1 tablespoon lucuma powder
- 1 teaspoon chaga mushroom extract powder
- ½ teaspoon vanilla powder
- ¼ teaspoon ground cinnamon
- ¼ teaspoon ground cardamom
- a pinch of sea salt

Drinking a chaga latte in the morning will give you energy without crashing and burning later. It is a perfect coffee replacement drink.

Put the cashew nuts into a bowl, pour in enough cold water to cover, and soak for 30 minutes, then drain and discard the soaking water.

Put the cashew nuts into a blender with all the remaining ingredients and blend well. Pour into glasses and serve.

Matcha Latte

Serves 2

- 1½ cups (12 fl oz/350 ml) almond milk
- 1 tablespoon almond butter
- 1 tablespoon coconut oil or coconut butter
- 1 teaspoon matcha powder
- ½ teaspoon maca powder
- a pinch of sea salt flakes
- sweetener of your choice, to taste

Warm the almond milk in a saucepan over low heat or with the milk steamer of an espresso machine (if you have one), then pour into a blender, add the remaining ingredients, and blend until smooth. Pour into a glass and serve.

Super Coffee

Serves 2

- 1 cup (8 fl oz/250 ml) cold coffee or herbal coffee
- scant ½ cup (3½ fl oz/100 ml) almond milk
- 2 tablespoons raw cacao powder
- 1 tablespoon hemp seeds
- 1 tablespoon coconut cream or coconut butter
- 2 teaspoons lucuma powder
- ¾ teaspoon chaga mushroom extract powder
- ½ teaspoon vanilla powder
- ¼ teaspoon reishi mushroom powder
- English caramel or toffee-flavored liquid stevia, to taste

Put all the ingredients into a blender and blend well. Pour into a glass and serve.

Spring Recipes and Activities

Sprouting

Sprouts are a beautiful reminder of how life awakes from hibernation in the spring. Home-grown sprouts are easy and fun to prepare.

1. Rinse the seeds, grains, or beans of your choice in a strainer (sieve) and then discard any that do not look healthy.
2. Put the seeds, grains, or beans into a sterilized glass jar and add water. The ratio of seeds to water should be 1:4. Instead of a lid, cover the jar with a piece of mesh (from inorganic fabric) and secure with a rubber band. Let sit overnight.
3. The next day, rinse the seeds, grains, or beans. Do this by turning the jar upside down and letting the water drip out, then fill it up with fresh cold water and let drip upside down again.
4. Next, put the jar on a drying rack, facing upside down, for an hour to drain the seeds. Let the jar sit for 3–6 days on the rack, rinsing twice a day with water as described above. For the first 2 days cover the jars with a cloth to keep the light out, then for the last few days, let the sprouts have light so that the leaves can produce chlorophyll.
5. When the sprouts are ready, put them into a bowl filled with water; after a while the husks should float to the top and can be removed easily.
6. Dry the sprouts with paper towels or a clean dish cloth, then put them into an airtight container and store in the refrigerator.
7. The sprouts will keep for up to a week if you wash and rinse them every 3 days and let them dry before storing again. A good rule is to smell the sprouts to check if they are okay to eat. Sprouts should smell fresh, not moldy.

TYPE	VOLUME OF SEEDS FOR 1 QUART (34-FL OZ/1–LITER) JAR	SOAKING TIME, HOURS	SPROUTING TIME, DAYS
adzuki beans	scant ½ cup (2¾ oz/75 g)	8	3–5
alfalfa seeds	2 tablespoons	10	4–6
amaranth	1¼ cups (9 oz/250 g)	8	2–3
buckwheat (with husk)	1½ cups (9 oz/250 g)	6–8	1–2, then follow instructions for growing indoor greens, page 193–4
buckwheat (without husk)	1½ cups (9 oz/250 g)	4	1–2
broccoli seeds	2–3 tablespoons	6–8	3–5
chickpeas	generous 1 cup (9 oz/250 g)	12	3–5
fenugreek seeds	scant ½ cup (2¾ oz/75 g)	10	4–6
green peas	1¼ cups (9 oz/250 g)	8	3–4
lentils	¾ cup (6 oz/175 g)	8	3–4
mung beans	¾ cup (4 oz/125 g)	8	3–4
quinoa	generous ¾ cup (4 oz/125 g)	4	1–2
radish seeds	3 tablespoons	6–8	4–6
sesame seeds	1⅔ cups (9 oz/250 g)	6	1–2
sunflower seeds with husk	1⅓ cups (7 oz/200 g)	6–8	1–2, then follow instructions for growing indoor greens, page 193–4
sunflower seeds without husk	1¾ cups (9 oz/250 g)	4–6	2–3
whole rye kernels	1⅓ cups (9 oz/250 g)	6–8	3–5
whole spelt kernels	1⅓ cups (9 oz/250 g)	6–8	3–5
whole wheat kernels	1⅓ cups (9 oz/250 g)	6–8	3–5

Growing Food On a Small Scale

Spring is the season of hope and new energy. Everything starts coming to life again after the long winter hibernation, so it's the perfect time to make plans for growing a few edible vegetables. Growing your own vegetables is a great way to connect with nature and feel the circle of life. If you have a tiny backyard, garden, balcony, or even just a kitchen windowsill, you can always find a vegetable that you will be able to grow.

It's best to start small anyway—try growing a few herbs on the windowsill, or buy a strawberry plant, plant it in a container, and watch the pretty white flowers turn into juicy red delicious strawberries. If you have some space outside, you can try growing your favorite vegetables in a deep pot or even in a large sturdy shopping bag. Hildur and I find that the only problem with small-scale gardening is that the harvest might feel too precious to eat.

Carrots

- a deep flower pot or container
- light, sandy soil or good organic soil mix (compost)
- 1 package of carrot seeds
- organic liquid fertilizer

In Iceland carrots are best sown in late spring (May) but in warmer places you can start earlier, just after the last frost.

Begin by preparing the flower pot or container. The pot or container needs to be deep enough for the roots to grow down and there needs to be drainage holes in the bottom of the pot or container so the carrots don't get waterlogged. Put the pot or container into a dish so the excess water will leak into the dish. Alternatively, if you can't make any drainage holes, then place some pumice or other stones in the bottom before adding the soil mix (compost) or soil. This will make room for any excess water.

Now we are ready to sow. Find the sunniest place available to position the flower pot or container. Fill it with light slightly sandy soil, then make ½–¾-inch (1–2-cm) deep furrows (drills) or rows (strips), every ⅝ inch (1.5 cm) from each other. Then sow the small carrot seeds thinly in the rows and cover very, very lightly with more soil. Water. Keep the soil moist and in about 3 weeks you will see some carrot leaves peeking up. When this happens, you need to thin the plants out. This is important so every root will have enough space to grow. About 1¾ inches (4 cm) is enough between roots. Water when the soil appears dry and add an organic liquid fertilizer to the water now and again. You can harvest all your carrots at once in about 10 weeks, or pick a few as they grow.

Beets

- for cold climates: small paper flower pots for presowing
- deep flower pot(s), at least 8 inches (20 cm) deep
- light soil, slightly alkaline (pH 6.5–7)
- a few beet (beetroot) seeds
- organic liquid fertilizer

Get ready to start after the last frost. Because of the cold weather conditions in Iceland it is good to presow beet (beetroot) seeds in small paper seedling pots and keep them inside while they germinate, lightly covered. When the leaves are sturdy (after a few weeks), we transfer the beets to bigger and deeper pots. If you live in a warmer climate, you can skip this and sow straight into the big pot(s). The big pot(s) should have drainage holes in the bottom so the beets don't get waterlogged. Put the pot into a dish so any excess water will leak into the dish.

Soak the beet seeds for a few hours before sowing. Meanwhile, fill your pot(s) with soil, blended with some organic fertilizer. Sow seed clusters about 1 inch (2.5 cm) deep and 2 inches (5 cm) apart. Lightly cover with soil. Keep the soil damp until germination. It can be useful to cover them lightly with a floating row cover (gardening fleece). The seeds should germinate in 5–10 days if the soil is kept moist. Thin the seedlings shortly after germination to give each plant space to develop and only keep the strongest seedling from each cluster. After about 3 weeks, when the leaves are becoming sturdy (about 2 inches/5 cm high) it is time to do the final thinning. Keep individual plants about 4 inches (10 cm) apart, or, if you did a presow in small pots, now is the time to transfer them to the big pot(s), keeping the same space between plants.

Keep an eye on the soil: When it appears dry, water it and add an organic liquid fertilizer to the water now and again. You can expect to start harvesting about 2 months after sowing. The leaves are edible (the smaller ones taste the best) and are great for salads and smoothies. It is okay to pick a few leaves from time to time before harvesting the root itself.

Healthy Easter Eggs

Makes 4 whole eggs

For the chocolate
- ¾ cup (6 fl oz/175 ml) coconut oil
- ¾ cup (6 oz/175 g) almond butter
- ½ cup (5¼ oz/160 g) coconut nectar or maple syrup
- ¾ cup (3¼ oz/90 g) raw cacao powder
- ⅓ cup (1 oz/30 g) lucuma powder
- ½ teaspoon maca powder
- ½ teaspoon cayenne pepper
- ¼ teaspoon sea salt flakes

For the crunch
- 2 tablespoons goji berries
- 2 tablespoons mulberries
- 2 tablespoons pumpkin seeds
- 2 tablespoons buckwheat sprouts
- 1 tablespoon chia seeds

To finish
- 2 tablespoons cacao butter
- 2 teaspoons raw cacao powder

There are different size Easter egg molds to choose from, but we love the small ones. For a nut-free version, use tahini instead of almond butter.

To make the chocolate, melt the coconut oil by placing the jar in a bowl filled with warm water.

Meanwhile put the almond butter and coconut nectar into a food processor and process to a smooth paste. Add the cacao powder and melted coconut oil and blend. Add the lucuma powder, maca powder, cayenne pepper, and sea salt flakes and blend well. Transfer the mixture to a large bowl, add all the ingredients for the crunch, and stir together until everything is combined.

Pour the chocolate mixture into 8 half Easter egg molds. Place in the freezer for 1 hour or in the refrigerator overnight, until they have hardened.

Once the egg halves have hardened, to make them into whole eggs, put the cacao butter into a heatproof bowl set over a saucepan of gently simmering water until melted, then remove from the heat and stir in the cacao powder until smooth. Brush the mixture over the edge of one of the egg halves and gently press the other half onto it to seal. Let stand for about 10 minutes, or until dried. Alternatively, leave as egg halves.

Tip: If you are not following a raw diet you can use maple syrup instead of coconut nectar if you like.

Spring Recipes and Activities

Hildur's Rhubarb Jam

Makes about 3¼ lb (1.5 kg)

- 2¼ lb (1 kg) rhubarb stalks, chopped into pieces
- 3½ cups (1 lb 2 oz/500 g) hulled and chopped strawberries
- scant 1 cup (7 oz/200 g) coconut palm sugar
- 2 tablespoons lemon juice
- 3 inch (7.5 cm) piece fresh ginger root, peeled
- 2 vanilla beans (pods)
- 1 cinnamon stick
- 1½ tablespoons ground chia seeds

Rhubarb grows vigorously in many backyards and gardens in spring and early summer. It is wonderful to use the very first stalks immediately, before they get too big and sturdy. The young stalks taste better and are healthier, because they contain less oxalic acid than older ones. Eating too much oxalic acid can prevent iron and calcium absorption in the body. Picking thin stalks in early spring benefits the rhubarb plant, too, and may mean that you can get a second harvest in the fall (autumn). The leaves cannot be eaten but they can be used for dyeing cloth or in recipes for making natural pesticides to use on the plants in the garden.

Put the fruit in a bowl with the coconut palm sugar and lemon juice and let stand for 30 minutes to infuse.

Put the fruit, any liquid in the bowl, and all the remaining ingredients, except the chia seeds, into a heavy suacepan and bring to a boil over medium heat. Boil for 10–15 minutes, stirring almost constantly to prevent the mixture from burning on the bottom of the pan. Remove the pan from the heat, stir in the chia seeds, then put back on the heat, bring to a boil again, and keep boiling for another 5–10 minutes, skimming off any foam from the top of the jam with a slotted spoon.

When the jam has thickened and starts to set, pour it into sterilized (see page 22) glass jars, let cool, and then seal with lids. This jam will keep in a cold place for 2–3 months. You can also freeze the jam in small portions.

Rhubarb and Apple Compote Layered Dessert

Serves 6–8

For the rhubarb layer
- 1 lb 2 oz (500 g) rhubarb stalks, cut into ¾-inch (2-cm) thick slices
- 1¾ cups (9 oz/250 g) hulled and quartered strawberries,

For the crumbs
- 1 cup (5 oz/150 g) pecans
- 3½ oz (100 g) gluten-free crispbreads
- ⅓ cup (2 oz/50 g) mulberries
- scant ¼ cup (2 oz/50 g) coconut palm sugar

For the apple layer
- 1⅓ cups (11 oz/300 g) organic store-bought applesauce (apple puree)

For the coconut cream
- 1 x 14 fl oz (400 ml) can coconut milk
- 1 teaspoon vanilla extract

To serve
- ice cream or whipped cream (optional)

This delicious dessert is inspired by the rhubarb compote Grandma Hildur used to make every spring—it's an all-time family favorite.

Start by making the rhubarb layer. Put the fruit into a saucepan and bring to a boil over medium heat. Boil for 15–20 minutes, stirring frequently.

Meanwhile, for the crumbs, put the pecans, crispbreads, and mulberries into a food processor and process until the mixture resembles bread crumbs. Transfer the bread crumbs to a wok or a saucepan, add the coconut palm sugar, and dry-roast, stirring constantly, for about 5 minutes, or until golden.

To assemble the dessert, put a layer of the fruit into the bottom of a glass, then add a layer of crumbs. Add a layer of applesauce (apple puree), another layer of crumbs, and repeat the layers until everything has been used.

To make the coconut cream, put the coconut milk into a blender with the vanilla and blend. When blended, transfer to a cream whipper. Screw the charger on tightly, shake the whipper, and press out the cream on top of the dessert.

Alternatively, you can serve the dessert with ice cream or plain whipped cream.

Simple Two-Day Cleansing Menu

Shopping List
for 1 person for 2 days

- 1 bunch of kale
- 2 organic apples
- 1 cucumber
- ½ bunch of celery
- 2 limes
- 1 bunch of cilantro (coriander)
- 1 bottle Ginger Shot (see page 96)
- 1¾ cups (9 oz/250 g) frozen
  blueberries
- 1 avocado
- 1 lemon
- 1 red onion
- 3 beets (beetroots)
- 1 sweet potato
- 1 x 14 oz (400 g) can coconut milk
- flaxseeds
- sesame seeds
- pumpkin seeds
- 1 x 6 oz (170 g) jar almond butter
- herbal tea
- ground turmeric
- ground cardamom powder
- ground cumin
- salt
- curry paste
- cayenne pepper

Check your pantry before going shopping, because you may have some of these ingredients already, especially the spices, seeds, and tea.

At the end of the year, the festive season arrives with all its celebrations and temptations. Many of us indulge in delicacies in larger quantities than we usually would, which is wonderful, as long as we feel good. But as the winter months draw to a close, we may start to feel that we have had too much fun and then have a hard time getting back into a healthy routine. To those people who have never struggled with this, congratulations, that's great news. But for others, they may well have experienced this kind of struggle. To get back into a healthy routine come springtime, follow this two-day menu of easily digested and mildly cleansing foods. It is a way of resetting the taste buds, getting rid of cravings, and helping to make the winter treats move faster through the digestive system. If you follow this plan, then the healthy routine will feel like a feast.

While on this plan, make sure that you are eating enough during the day so you can focus and keep your energy levels up; you should not be starving during this time. Choose days to do this plan when you aren't busy or you don't have to work. It's best when you have time to relax, do some yoga or meditation, take peaceful walks, or do something that calms your mind.

This menu is composed of a green juice, smoothie, soup, and homemade crackers. Please have as many servings as you feel you need and remember to drink water and herbal tea during the day when you are thirsty. The ingredients list in the recipes are not too long and we have included a shopping list so you can buy all your ingredients before getting started. All the recipes are easy to make and we recommend making them in large batches before you start, so you can spend your two days relaxing and enjoying the journey.

Green Juice

Serves 2

- 1 handful of kale, stems (stalks) removed and leaves chopped into small pieces
- ½–1 apple, cored and chopped into small pieces
- ½ cucumber, chopped into small pieces
- 2 celery stalks, chopped into small pieces
- 1 lime, quartered
- ½ bunch of cilantro (coriander)
- 1 tablespoon Ginger Shot (see page 96)

You can use whatever greens you prefer: kale, spinach, or another favorite vegetable. Chopping the fruit and vegetables into small pieces will make the blending easier as well as preserve more nutrients.

Put all the ingredients into a blender with scant ½–scant 1 cup (3½–7 fl oz/100–200 ml) water and blend well. Strain through a nut milk bag or a piece of cheesecloth (muslin) set over a bowl, then pour into a glass and drink. Set the pulp still in the nut milk bag or cheesecloth (muslin) aside and use it for the smoothie (see below) and the crackers (see page 70).

"Green" Smoothie

Serves 2

- 1¼ cups (10 fl oz/300 ml) herbal tea
- 2 tablespoons pulp from the Green Juice (see above)
- 2 cups (11 oz/300 g) frozen blueberries
- ½ avocado
- 1 tablespoon almond butter
- 2 tablespoons Ginger Shot (see page 96)
- 1 tablespoon lemon juice
- ½ teaspoon ground turmeric
- ½ teaspoon ground cardamom powder
- a pinch of salt

Use your favourite herbal tea in this smoothie. We like cinnamon and star anise. For a nut-free version, use tahini instead of almond butter.

Put all the ingredients into a blender and blend well. Pour into a glass and drink.

Tip: Use sesame seed paste (tahini) instead of the almond butter if you prefer not to use nuts.

Pulp Crackers

Serves 2

- scant 1 cup (5 oz/150 g) flaxseeds
- scant 1 cup (7 fl oz/200 ml) pulp from the Green Juice (see page 68)
- 1 cup (5 oz/150 g) sesame seeds
- generous ¾ cup (3½ oz/100 g) pumpkin seeds
- ½ teaspoon salt
- 2 tablespoons your favorite curry paste

Put the flaxseeds into a bowl, then pour in 1¼ cups (10 fl oz/300 ml) water, and soak for 30 minutes. All the water should be absorbed.

Preheat the oven to 410°F/210°C/Gas Mark 6½ and line a baking sheet with parchment (baking) paper.

Put all the ingredients into a bowl and stir together to form a dough. Spread the dough evenly over the prepared sheet and press down; it should be ¼ inch (½ cm) thick. Bake for 30–35 minutes. Remove from the oven and let cool.

Alternatively, if you prefer to use a dehydrator, place the dough onto a Teflex sheet, spread it out evenly, and score into your desired shape using a pizza roller or a knife. Dehydrate for 10–12 hours at 105°F/40°C, then flip the crackers over and remove the Teflex sheet. Continue to dehydrate for 6–8 hours, or until crispy and dry.

Once cool, brake the crackers into squares and store in a air tight container for up to 2 months.

Beet and Sweet Potato Soup

Serves 2

- 1 teaspoon olive oil
- 1 red onion, thinly sliced
- 2 teaspoons ground cumin
- ¾ teaspoon ground turmeric
- ½–1 teaspoon salt
- ¼ teaspoon cayenne pepper
- 3 beets (beetroots), peeled and diced
- 1 sweet potato, peeled and diced
- scant 1 cup (7 fl oz/200 ml) coconut milk

Warm the oil in a saucepan over medium-low heat, add the onion, and cook gently for about 10 minutes, or until soft. Be careful not to burn the onion. Add the spices and all the remaining ingredients, then pour in 3½ cups (27 fl oz/800 ml) water and simmer for 45–60 minutes, or until all the vegetables are cooked. Transfer the mixture to a blender and blend until smooth. Serve.

Midmorning

Snacks

On the Go

—

Summer Recipes and Activities

Most of us regularly dine away from home and reluctantly buy food in a hurry that doesn't really fit into a healthy lifestyle. With some foresight, organization, and creativity, it doesn't have to be time consuming to make delicious healthy meals to go, and most of the time it will also save money. The quickest and cheapest way is to use leftovers, which also helps to reduce food waste. When we do have time, it is incredibly rewarding to make something tasty from scratch, and often we make our life easier by preparing food a few days ahead.

In addition to what we eat, it is also important to think about how we eat. Hildur and I encourage everyone who's used to eating on the run, in the car, or in front of the computer screen at work to take time to enjoy the food they are eating. Make lunch a pleasurable time to sit down, enjoy, and notice how our bodies feel about the food we're eating. This way we can sense how much we need to eat, as well as get more delight and enjoyment from our meals. We will also become more satisfied and start to have fewer cravings for candies and other sweet things.

Gluten-Free Crackers

Makes about 20 crackers

- ½ cup (2½ oz/65 g) gluten-free flour mix
- ¾ cup (2¾ oz/70 g) almond flour
- 2 tablespoons ground chia seeds
- 2 tablespoons sesame seeds
- 1 tablespoon nutritional yeast flakes
- 1 teaspoon dried rosemary needles
- ½ teaspoon sea salt flakes
- ½ teaspoon dried thyme
- ¼ teaspoon garlic powder
- ¼ teaspoon baking powder
- 1 teaspoon extra virgin olive oil

These simple crackers taste great with Pistachio and Kale Hummus (see page 82) or Almond Butter and Herb Hummus (see page 80).

Preheat the oven to 350°F/180°C/Gas Mark 4.

Start by mixing all the dry ingredients together in a large bowl. Add ⅓ cup (2½ fl oz/75 ml) water and the oil slowly. Don't add all the water at once; it is best to add it gradually, because you may not need it all. Knead the dough with your hands until it comes together into a ball.

Place the dough between 2 sheets of parchment (baking) paper and roll out until it is ⅛ inch/3 mm thick. Peel off the top sheet and place the bottom sheet with the dough on top onto a baking sheet. Using a pizza wheel, cut the dough into 2 inch (5 cm) squares. This makes it easier to break into pieces after baking. Bake for 20–25 minutes, then cool on the baking sheet and break into pieces. The crackers can be stored in an airtight container for up to 1 month.

Homemade Cashew Nut Cheese Spread

Makes 10–15 balls

- 2 cups (11 oz/300 g) cashew nuts
- powder from 3 probiotic capsules
- 4 tablespoons lemon juice
- 2 tablespoons coconut oil, plus extra for oiling
- 2 tablespoons nutritional yeast flakes
- 1½ teaspoons organic apple cider vinegar
- 1 teaspoon salt

For mix 1
- 3 tablespoons pistachios
- 3 tablespoons cranberries
- 2 tablespoons minced red onion
- 1 teaspoon sea salt flakes
- pinch black pepper

For mix 2
- 3 tablespoons wasabi sesame seeds
- 1 tablespoon black sesame seeds

Put the cashew nuts into a bowl, pour in enough water to cover, and soak for at least 2 hours. Drain and discard the soaking water.

Put the cashew nuts into a blender with all the remaining ingredients and blend well. You may need to stop a few times and scrape the sides down with a rubber spatula. If you don't have a powerful blender, you can use a food processor. You will need to stop a few times to scrape down the sides. The mixture should resemble extra thick mashed potatoes and be free from any lumps. Transfer the mixture to a bowl, cover with plastic wrap (clingfilm), and chill in the refrigerator for about 5 hours, or overnight.

Before making the balls, lightly oil your hands. This will keep the mixture from sticking to your hands while you roll. Choose a mix, spread it out in a shallow bowl, then, using your hands, divide the cashew nut mixture into 15 small or 10 large balls and roll them in the mix until coated. The balls can be stored in an airtight container for 7–10 days.

Raw Almond and Rosemary Crackers

Makes about 30 crackers

- 2 cups (11 oz/300 g) almonds
- ¼ cup (1½ oz/40 g) ground chia seeds
- 2 tablespoons nutritional yeast flakes
- 1 teaspoon sea salt flakes
- ¼ teaspoon ground black pepper
- 2 tablespoons dried rosemary

Put the almonds into a bowl, pour in enough water to cover, and soak overnight. Drain and discard the soaking water.

Put the almonds into a food processor and process until it is a coarse meal (flour). Add the ground chia seeds, nutritional yeast flakes, sea salt, and black pepper and pulse to combine. With the food processor running slowly, add 6 tablespoons water and the rosemary down the feed tube. Stop and scrape down the sides with a rubber spatula. Turn the machine back on and add a little more water until the mixture is thick, looks like oatmeal (porridge), and is easy to spread. Use a rubber spatula to spread the mixture onto a nonstick sheet, such as Teflex, placed on a baking sheet or dehydrator tray. Using a sharp knife, gently score the mixture into cracker shapes, then put the tray or sheet into the dehydrator. Set the dehydrator to 145°F/63°C and let dehydrate for 1 hour. Reduce the heat to 118°F/48°C and dehydrate until the crackers are ready. This can take 8–12 hours, depending on how thick or thin the mixture has been spread out over the sheets.

Alternatively, preheat the oven to its lowest setting and place in the oven with the door ajar. Heat for 8 hours, or until crisp and dry.

Almond Butter and Herb Hummus

Serves 10

- 1⅔ cups (14 oz/400 g) can chickpeas, rinsed
- 2 tablespoons almond butter
- ¼ cup (2 fl oz/60 ml) lemon juice
- 2 cloves garlic
- ½ teaspoon wasabi sesame seeds
- ½ teaspoon thyme
- ½ teaspoon sea salt flakes
- 1 bunch of cilantro (coriander), chopped
- ¼ cup (2 fl oz/60 ml) olive oil
- crackers, to serve

To garnish
- ½ tablespoon extra virgin olive oil
- 1–2 teaspoons za'atar

Put the chickpeas into a food processor, add the almond butter, lemon juice, garlic, sesame seeds, thyme, and sea salt and blend well. Add the cilantro (coriander), then while the food processor is running, slowly pour in the olive oil down the feed tube until it is combined. Transfer to a serving dish, drizzle with the olive oil, and sprinkle with the za'atar. Serve with crackers.

Pistachio
and Kale Hummus

Serves 10

- 1½ cups (9 oz/250 g) cooked chickpeas
- ½ cup (2½ oz/60 g) shelled pistachios
- 2 kale leaves, stems (stalks) removed
- ¼ cup (½ oz/15 g) basil leaves, chopped
- ¼ cup (2 fl oz/60 ml) lemon juice
- 2 tablespoons grated lemon zest
- ¼ cup (2 fl oz/60 ml) olive oil
- 2 cloves garlic
- 1 teaspoon sea salt
- 1 teaspoon cayenne pepper
- crackers, to serve

To garnish
- 1½ teaspoons extra virgin olive oil
- 2 teaspoons sesame seeds

Put all the ingredients into a food processor and blend until smooth, scraping down the sides of the blender with a rubber spatula when needed. Transfer to a serving dish, drizzle with the olive oil, and sprinkle with the chopped pistachios. Serve with crackers.

Salad in a Jar for When You are on the Go

Serves 1

For the dressing
- ¼ cup (2 fl oz/60 ml) favorite cold-pressed oil
- 1 orange, peeled
- 1 lime, peeled
- ¼ cup (15 g/½ oz) basil leaves
- 3–4 dates, pitted
- 1 tablespoon mustard
- 1 teaspoon red pepper (chili) flakes
- ½ teaspoon sea salt flakes

For the salad
- 2 tablespoons chopped red onions
- ¼ cup (1½ oz/40 g) finely shaved fennel
- 1 corn cob, cooked and kernels removed
- 1 carrot, very thinly sliced
- ½ cup (3¼ oz/90 g) cooked quinoa
- ½ cup (1 oz/30 g) cooked cannellini beans
- ½ cup (2¼ oz/60 g) marinated tofu or ½ cup (2¾ oz/75 g) feta cheese or ½ cup (2¾ oz/75 g) cubed avocado
- 10 black olives, pitted (optional)
- ¼ cup (1½ oz/45 g) pomegranate seeds
- 1 cup (1 oz/25 g) shredded kale leaves (about 4 leaves)
- 2 tablespoons roasted pumpkin seeds

The key to this salad is to put the dressing in the bottom of the jar; that way the salad can be kept in the refrigerator for up to 2 days until you are ready to eat it. If you are using onions, put them on the bottom, because soaking them in the dressing makes them soft and sweet. It's best to put the ingredients that absorb the least fluid, such as fennel, corn, and carrot directly on top of the dressing. Then, add the beans, grains, or tofu and continue to layer your salad with dried or fresh fruit. It is important to put the greens on top, because that prevents the salad from becoming soggy. If you include nuts, seeds, or cheese, add these last. Avocados and tomatoes are best put in the jar the morning of the day you will be eating your salad, otherwise they may spoil. Place the filled jar in the refrigerator and you are good to go.

To enjoy, just tip the salad into a bowl and toss the ingredients until everything is well mixed and coated with the dressing.

For the dressing, put all the ingredients into a blender and blend until smooth.

Put the dressing at the bottom of a clean 1 quart (34 fl oz/1 liter) glass jar, then add the onions, fennel, corn, and carrot. Add the quinoa, beans, tofu, olives (if using), pomegranate seeds, kale, pumpkin seeds, and feta or avocado (if using).

Tip: If you are following a vegan diet, use tofu or avocado in your salad rather than the feta cheese.

Superfood Energy Bars

Makes 14 bars

- 1 cup (5 oz/150 g) almonds
- ½ cup (1 oz/30 g) coconut flakes
- ½ cup (3 oz/80 g) pumpkin seeds
- ½ cup (2¾ oz/70 g) hemp seeds
- ¼ cup (1 oz/25 g) goji berries
- ¼ cup (1½ oz/40 g) chia seeds
- ¼ cup (2½ oz/60 g) almond butter
- ¼ cup (2¾ oz/75 g) coconut oil
- ¼ cup (1 oz/30 g) mulberries
- ¼ cup (1 oz/25 g) cacao nibs
- 5 oz/150 g dates, pitted
- 1 teaspoon red pepper (chili) flakes
- 1 teaspoon sea salt flakes
- 1 tablespoon Homemade Energy Mix (see page 22)

Homemade energy bars are so simple and easy to make. Don't be discouraged by the long list of ingredients here. All you have to do is to mix, mold, cool, and enjoy. We always have these energy bars ready in the freezer or refrigerator, so that we can easily grab one after a workout, before a bike ride, or as a snack while we are busy.

Line an 8 x 8 inch (20 x 20 cm) baking pan with parchment (baking) paper and set aside.

Put the almonds, coconut flakes, pumpkin seeds, hemp seeds, goji berries, and chia seeds into a food processor and process until the almonds have become crumbs. Add all the remaining ingredients and blend until it sticks together.

Spread the mixture evenly over the bottom of the lined baking pan and press it into the pan. Chill in the refrigerator for at least 2–3 hours. We like to cut it into bars before putting into the refrigerator.

Stored in an airtight container, the bars will keep for 3 weeks in the refrigerator and up to 2 months in the freezer.

Round Rice Snacks

Makes 6 rice snacks

- ½ avocado, peeled and cut into cubes
- 1 tablespoon lime juice
- 1 cup (6 oz/175 g) cooked short-grain brown rice
- 3 tablespoons toasted sesame seeds, plus extra for coating
- 1 teaspoon black sesame seeds (optional)
- 1 teaspoon tamari
- ¼–½ teaspoon sea salt flakes
- 3 chives, finely chopped
- 6 slices pickled ginger
- 1 quantity Spicy Mayo (see page 92)

These round rice delights resemble fast-food snacks that Hildur once had at a Japanese gas station—if only fast food was always this exciting. These snacks are perfect to take on long bike rides or hikes in the countryside, because the carbohydrates in the rice provide plenty of good energy while you are on the go.

Put the avocado into a nonreactive bowl and pour over the lime juice. Set aside.

Put the rice, sesame seeds, tamari, sea salt flakes, and finely chopped chive into a food processor and press the pulse button several times, or until the rice becomes sticky.

Line a small dessert bowl with plastic wrap (clingfilm), letting it hang over the sides. Place 2 tablespoons of the rice mixture into the bowl, then add a piece of avocado in the middle along with a piece of pickled ginger and ½ teaspoon of the spicy mayo. Place 1 tablespoon of the rice mixture on top, then gather up the plastic wrap, make a twist at the top, and lift the rice out of the bowl and shape into a ball. Remove the plastic wrap and place the ball in the palm of your hand to finish shaping it into a ball. Repeat until all the rice mixture is used.

Put some extra sesame seeds onto a plate and roll the rice balls, one by one, in the seeds to coat. They are ready to eat.

Millet Bowl to Go

Serves 2

- ⅔ cup (3½ oz/100 g) pecans
- ⅔ cup (3½ oz/100 g) florets cauliflower
- 1 tablespoon vegan barbecue sauce
- a handful of cilantro (coriander)
- a handful of mint, chopped
- a handful of flat-leaf parsley
- 3½ oz/100 g cherry tomatoes, halved
- ½ cucumber, seeded and thinly sliced
- ¼ red onion, thinly sliced
- ⅓ cup (2 oz/50 g) dried mulberries
- seeds from 1 pomegranate
- 2 tablespoons capers
- 2 tablespoons lime zest
- 2–3 tablespoons Wild Sorrel Pesto (see page 144), optional

For the millet
- generous ⅓ cup (2¾ oz/75 g) millet
- 1 teaspoon fennel seeds
- 1 tablespoon olive oil
- pinch of sea salt flakes

Start by cooking the millet. In a saucepan, dry-roast the millet with the fennel seeds for about 5 minutes, or until it turns golden. Keep an eye on it, because it may burn easily. Pour in ¾ cup (6 fl oz/175 ml) water, then add the olive oil and season with sea salt flakes, stir, and bring it to a boil. Reduce the heat and simmer for about 15 minutes. Turn off the heat and let the pan stand for 10 minutes. Using 2 forks, fluff up the millet, and it's ready to eat.

Meanwhile, preheat the broiler (grill).

Put the pecans into a skillet or frying pan and dry-roast over medium heat for about 5 minutes, or until aromatic. Remove from the heat and coarsely chop, then set aside.

Rub the cauliflower florets in the barbecue sauce, put on a broiler (grill) pan, and broil (grill) for 2–3 minutes.

Arrange all the remaining ingredients in a large bowl, starting with the millet and mixing with the chopped herbs. Then add the cauliflower, tomatoes, cucumber, onion, pecans, mulberries, pomegranate seeds, capers, and finally sprinkle with the lime zest. Top with the pesto, if using, and enjoy.

Sushi Wrap

Makes 2 wraps

- 2 nori sheets
- 1 handful of lettuce, kale, or spinach
- 1 cup (6½ oz/185 g) cooked quinoa
- 1 avocado, peeled, pitted, and thinly sliced
- ½ sweet potato, baked and peeled
- ½ mango, peeled and thinly sliced
- 2 tablespoons chopped cilantro (coriander)
- 4–5 chives

For the spicy mayo
- 1⅓ cups (7 oz/200 g) cashew nuts
- 3 dates, pitted
- 2 tablespoons lemon juice
- ½–1 tablespoon vegan sambal oelek or other chili paste
- 1 clove garlic
- 1 teaspoon onion powder
- ½–1 teaspoon wasabi powder
- a pinch of sea salt
- freshly ground black pepper

For the rhubarb
- 2 rhubarb stalks, thinly sliced
- 1 teaspoo vegan sambal oelek
- 1 teaspoon coconut palm sugar
- pinch of sea salt flakes

This recipe is excellent for using up leftover veggies. If you don't have any leftover sweet potatoes, then roast some carrots or use raw ones, very thinly sliced.

For the spicy mayo, put the cashew nuts into a bowl, pour in enough water to cover, and soak for 2 hours. Drain and discard the soaking water.

Put the cashew nuts into a blender, pour in scant ½ cup (3½ fl oz/100 ml) water, add the remaining ingredients, and blend until combined. Set aside.

To make the rhubarb, cook it with the sambal olek, coconut palm sugar, and sea salt flakes in a saucepan over medium heat for 3–4 minutes, or until golden. Set aside.

Place a nori sheet, shiny side up, onto a bamboo rolling mat. Cover two-thirds of the nori sheet with lettuce, leaving one-third from the bottom edge free. Be sure to have at least 1¼ inches (3 cm) free at the bottom of the sheet (on the right side) so you can close the roll. Spread the quinoa on top of the lettuce, pressing it down and making sure that the layer is ¼ inch (½ cm) thick. Arrange the avocado, sweet potatoes or carrots, rhubarb, and mango in a thin horizontal line down the middle of the quinoa. Arrange the cilantro (coriander) and chives on top of the vegetables and add some of the spicy mayo, then start rolling up the near end, using the bamboo mat to help you. When the roll is nearly complete, fold up the "empty" bottom edge of the nori sheet on the right to keep the filling inside the roll. Spread a little spicy mayo onto the ends to seal the roll. Repeat with the remaining nori, quinoa, and vegetables.

Cauliflower Patties

Serves 4–6

- 1 head cauliflower,
  cut into small florets
- 1 teaspoon smoked paprika
- 1 teaspoon thyme
- 1 tablespoon olive oil
- ⅓ cup (2½ oz/60 g) millet, cooked
- 1 cup (6 oz/175 g) cooked
  chickpeas
- ¾ cup (2¼ oz/60 g) vegan
  Parmesan-style cheese
- a handful of cilantro (coriander)
- 3 scallions (spring onions),
  chopped
- ¼ cup (1½ oz/40 g) ground
  chia seeds
- 2 teaspoons green curry paste
- ½–1 teaspoon sea salt flakes
- ½ teaspoon freshly ground
  black pepper

To serve
- Fermented Beet (see page 157)
- 1 lime, quartered
- cress or corn salad (mâche),
  for sprinkling
- Spicy Mayo (see page 92)
  or homemade raita
  (see page 44), optional

Preheat the oven to 400°F/200°C/Gas Mark 6. Line 2 baking sheets with parchment (baking) paper.

Put the cauliflower onto the lined baking sheet, season with the smoked paprika, thyme, and olive oil and roast in the oven for 10 minutes. Keep the oven on.

Put the cooked millet into a food processor, press the pulse button, and pulse several times, or until the millet starts to become a little sticky. Add all the remaining ingredients to the food processor, including the cauliflower, and pulse everything together. Don't overdo it—the texture should be sticky but not too mushy.

Using clean hands, divide the mixture into about 8 medium balls, and flatten with the palms of your hands into patties. Put the patties onto the other lined baking sheet and bake in the oven for 8 minutes. Turn them over and bake for another 5 minutes. They should be golden on both sides.

Serve with some fermented beet (beetroot) and a lime wegde and sprinkle with cress.

Tip: These patties are also delicious when served with spicy mayo or homemade raita.

Green Tea and Ginger Soda

Makes 4¼ cups (34 fl oz/1 liter)

- 4¼ cups (34 fl oz/1 liter) sparkling water
- 2 tablespoons Ginger Shot (see below)
- 1 tablespoon lemon juice
- 1 teaspoon matcha powder
- sprigs of fresh thyme, to serve (optional)

For the ginger shot
- 5 inch (13.25 cm) or about 7 oz (200 g) piece fresh ginger root, peeled

This homemade soda is our favorite pick-me-up energy drink when we need to concentrate and be productive. The green tea sharpens our mind and makes us more focused. This soda is sugar free, too.

To make a ginger shot, put the ginger through a juicer or chop the ginger and put it into a blender with 1–2 tablespoons water and blend until smooth.

Pour the sparkling water into a clean bottle, add the ginger shot, lemon juice, and matcha powder. Carefully stir and enjoy.

Summer Recipes and Activities

Coloring with Natural Dyes

How to Dye Cloth Summer Yellow

When we are mindful of treating our bodies well by eating healthily and of caring about the environment by buying organic, local foods, we often feel inspired to transfer these ideas to other areas as well. One thing Hildur and I love to do is to experiment with flowers, spices, and foods that can give color to fabrics. We love the idea of using something natural and edible to dye the fabrics that lie next to our skin. These fabrics can then be used for making clothes, dish towels, blankets, cloths, or whatever else you can think of. There are so many wonderful colors that can be produced by using natural sources.

In the summer, we have a range of flowers and herbs in our garden that can be used in coloring projects. Garden nasturtium (*Tropaeolum majus*) is one of our favorite flowers to grow as an edible for salads, and to use as a color source. Beet (beetroot) juice and turmeric root give wonderful colors, while onion skin, pomegranate rind, and rhubarb leaves are great examples of food scraps that can be used in dyeing projects. Such natural dyeing can be done all year round, but we love to do these projects in the summer and let the fabric dry outside on a string, in a light breeze.

- 1½ cups (5 oz/150 g) grated fresh turmeric
- 39 x 78 inch (100 x 200 cm) washed cotton cloth
- hemp string

Start by putting the grated turmeric into a piece of cheesecloth (muslin) or in a nut milk bag. Fill a 2 gallon (10 liter) pot two-thirds full of water and add the turmeric. Bring the water to a boil.

Meanwhile, rinse and drain the cloth, then let dry. When dry, use the hemp string to make as many pretty tie dye circles as desired. You just tie the string around the cloth here and there—however you want.

When the water starts boiling, add the cloth and let simmer for 25 minutes. Poke with a wooden spoon to be sure the cloth is covered with water. Turn off the heat and let stand for 15 minutes, then thoroughly rinse the cloth under cold water. Now you can untie the strings and admire your art. Wring out and hang up to dry.

Compost Guide for Small Spaces

We were both brought up with composting as a normal part of everyday life. Grandma Hildur and Grandpa Eiríkur viewed organic scraps from the kitchen as highly valuable, because they could be transformed into nutritious compost for the garden. This is the circle of life at work, and it is wonderful to watch and feel that we are a part of it. If you have a backyard or garden it is easy to find space for a compost bin or pile (heap), but even if you don't have an area outside you can still make your own soil, if you want to. Here is how to make compost for a small space.

Basics for a Healthy Compost

- Microbes and worms take care of breaking down all the kitchen scraps and dry material. They are the foundation for an effective compost, but you can add an "infection" from another active compost to help with the break down of the material. If you add soil from an active compost (one filled with good bacteria), it will "infect" your soil and help with the break-down work.

- It is very important to help the microbes access the material by chopping everything up into smaller pieces—this makes the surface area bigger and the turnover faster.

- Regular blending and stirring is important to get air into the compost.

- Keeping the moisture level balanced is key to a good healthy compost. Too wet = bad smell; too dry = slow breakdown. So water a dry compost and add more dry material to a wet compost.

- The following can go into the compost:
  All kitchen scraps from the plant kingdom (fruit bark, vegetable scraps, leftovers, coffee grounds, tea bags).
  The only item from the animal kingdom that can go in are eggshells.
  From the garden you can use leaves, hay, small branches, and most other things except weeds.

- The following cannot go into the compost:
  Animal food scraps (meat, bones, fish, milk, and other dairy) because they can attract pests (rats) and they also risk bad odor and unwanted microbes.

- It is a good idea to place the compost where it can get some sunlight, because heat helps the turnover.

- Have fun.

Instructions for Compost

- 1 x 5–10 gallon (5–10 liter) plastic box
- 2 lids
- drill, fitted with a ¼ inch (5 mm) drill bit
- 20–40 live worms
- "infection" from a lively compost (or some regular soil)
- dry material (dry leaves, shredded paper, shredded wood, and so on)

Start by deciding where to put the small compost bin. It can be on a patio or balcony.

Using the drill, carefully drill air holes into the bottom, sides, and one of the lids of the plastic box. Position the undrilled lid where you want the compost, then place the box on top and add some soil, live worms, and dry material to the box.

At this point you can start adding food scraps. It is important that everything is chopped into very small pieces.

Shake the box every day. Try to make sure that there is a balanced moisture level in the box by mixing everything up. Kitchen scraps give out moisture, while dry material (leaves, shredded paper, and so on) are dry and don't produce any moisture.

Check out the tips (left) for a healthy compost.

Ice Pops

We love making ice pops (lollies) from leftover smoothies and juices. That was how our ice pop-making started many, many years ago. Today, we also love to make them from scratch. In our family, kids and grown-ups alike love these refreshing frozen treats—especially in summer. For the kids, we make healthy alternatives to the store-bought ones that have a tendency to contain more sugar than is actually needed. For the grown-ups, we love to make the ice pops refreshing with a kick. Some of our favorites contain matcha powder or cold coffee.

Tofu Chocolate
Ice Pops for Children

Makes 8

- 3½ oz (100 g) soft (silken) tofu
- 1 banana
- 2 tablespoons raw cacao powder
- 2 tablespoons coconut palm sugar
- 1 cup (8 fl oz/250 ml) almond milk

Put all the ingredients into a blender and blend until smooth. Pour the mixture into ice pop (lolly) molds and freeze for at least 4 hours.

Matcha and Coconut Water
Ice Pops for Grown-Ups

Makes 6

- 1 cup (8 fl oz/250 ml) coconut water
- 3 kiwifruits, peeled
- 1 tablespoon sweetener of your choice
- 1 teaspoon matcha tea powder

Put all the ingredients into a blender and blend until smooth. Pour the mixture into ice pop (lolly) molds and freeze for at least 4 hours.

Adzuki and Almond Ice Pops

Makes 10

- 1 cup (9 oz/250 g) Adzuki Bean Paste (see page 210, just swap the black beans with adzuki beans)
- 1 cup (8 fl oz/250 ml) almond milk
- 1 tablespoon coconut oil
- ¼ cup (3 oz/80 g) coconut nectar or maple syrup
- 1 teaspoon lemon juice
- 1 teaspoon vanilla powder
- a pinch of salt

Put all the ingredients into a blender and blend until smooth. Pour the mixture into ice pop (lolly) molds and freeze for at least 4 hours.

Tip: This recipe uses a bean paste to give the mixture a smooth consistency, but you can also use the whole beans, if desired.

Picnic

On beautiful summer days, picnics are a great way to spend time with family and friends. Enjoy good food, fresh air, and the sunshine. When we eat outside in nature, food tastes different and everything is more enjoyable in good company.

We like to bring foods that can be served cold, but if you are having a picnic in your own yard or garden you can serve parts of the menu hot from the grill, such as the Grilled Sourdough Pizza (see page 118).

Tomato Salad with Dried Olives and Incan Berries

Serves 4

- 3½ oz (100 g) cucumber
- 1¾ cups (9 oz/250 g) cherry tomatoes, halved
- 2 avocados, peeled, pitted, and cut into cubes
- 2 celery stalks, very thinly sliced
- 3½ oz (100 g) sun-dried olives
- ⅔ cup (3½ oz/100 g) Incan golden berries
- 1 cup (3½ oz/100 g) sun-dried tomatoes in oil, drained
- ⅓ cup (2 oz/50 g) raw pine nuts
- 1 handful of basil, chopped
- 2–3 red or purple kale leaves, torn into pieces
- juice of 1 lemon
- 1–2 tablespoons cold-pressed olive oil
- a pinch of sea salt and freshly ground black pepper

Slice the cucumbers in half lengthwise and, using a spoon, scoop out the seeds and discard. Slice the flesh into ¼ inch (½ cm) pieces. Put the cucumber into a large serving bowl with the tomatoes, avocados, celery, sun-dried olives, Incan golden berries, sun-dried tomatoes, pine nuts, basil, and kale. Mix to combine, then add the lemon juice, olive oil, salt, and pepper, and toss together.

Tip: Lightly toast the pine nuts instead of using raw ones, if desired.

Kale Chips

Serves 4

- 1 bunch of kale, stems (stalks) removed and leaves torn into bite-size pieces

For the dressing
- 1 cup (5 oz/150 g) cashew nuts
- juice from 1 lime
- 2 tablespoons nutritional yeast flakes
- 1 tablespoon onion powder
- 2 dates, chopped
- 1 clove garlic
- ½ teaspoon red pepper (chili) flakes
- ½ teaspoon smoked paprika

For the dressing, put all the ingredients into a high-speed blender with about 4 tablespoons water and blend until smooth. (You might need to add a little more water if the dressing is too thick.)

Put the kale into a large bowl and pour over the dressing. Mix with your hands until the leaves are coated with the dressing. Spread the kale out on dehydrator trays, then put the trays into the dehydrator and set to 115°F/46°C. Dehydrate for 4–6 hours, or until crisp.

Alternatively, if you are not following a raw diet, place the kale on a baking sheet and bake at 275°F/140°C for 25 minutes, flipping over half way through.

The chips will keep for up to 4 weeks in a airtight container.

Spelt Calzone with Cilantro Chutney

Serves 4

For the dough
- 3½ cups (15½ oz/440 g) spelt flour
- 1–2 teaspoons aluminium-free baking powder
- 1 teaspoon sea salt flakes
- 1 teaspoon garlic powder
- 3 tablespoons olive oil

For the filling
- 1 cup (7 oz/200 g) baked sweet potatoes
- ½ cup (2¾ oz/75 g) tofu
- ¼ cup (1½ oz/40 g) toasted chopped pecans
- ¼ cup coriander chutney
- 1 teaspoon cayenne pepper
- salt

For the cilantro chutney
- ⅓ cup (½ oz/15 g) cilantro (coriander) leaves
- ¼ cup (⅛ oz/5 g) mint leaves
- ¾ inch (2 cm) piece of fresh ginger root, peeled and ground
- 1 green chile, chopped
- 1 tablespoon lemon juice
- zest of 1 lemon
- 1 cup (2¾ oz/70 g) toasted coconut flakes
- 1 clove garlic
- ½ teaspoon ground cumin
- ½ cup (4 fl oz/120 ml) olive oil
- sea salt

If you are not vegan, you can make the filling with feta cheese or goat cheese instead of tofu.

For the filling, put all the ingredients into a bowl and use your hands to mix everything together. Set aside.

To make the chutney, put all the ingredients into a food processor and blend together to combine. Transfer to a sterilized (see page 22) glass jar and cover with a lid. Set aside.

Preheat the oven to 400°F/200°C/Gas Mark 6.

Mix the spelt flour, baking powder, sea salt, and garlic powder together in a bowl. Make a well in the middle and add the olive oil. Start to mix, then slowly add 1⅓–1½ cups (11–12 fl oz/325–350 ml) lukewarm water, a little at a time, until it forms a dough. Shape the dough into a ball, then place it onto a lightly dusted work counter and knead for few minutes. The dough is ready when it starts to feel like your earlobe. Divide the dough into 4 equal portions.

Place a sheet of parchment (baking) paper on the work counter, place a dough portion on top, and, using a rolling pin, roll out to a circle about 1/16 inch (2 mm) thick. We like to use a dessert plate to form a circle around which we cut out the dough. Place a quarter of the filling on one half of the dough, then fold over the other half and pinch the edges together. Repeat with the remaining dough circles and filling.

Place the calzones onto a nonstick baking sheet and bake for 10 minutes, or until golden. Serve with the chutney.

Grilled Sourdough Pizza

Makes 2 medium pizzas

- ½ cup (3½ oz/100 g) ready-to-use sourdough starter (see below)
- scant ½ cup (3½ oz/100 g) yogurt with live cultures or vegan yogurt
- 1⅔ cups (7 oz/200 g) fine spelt flour, plus extra for dusting
- 1 teaspoon baking powder
- ¼ teaspoon sea salt
- 1 teaspoon olive oil

For the sourdough starter
- scant ½ cup (3½ fl oz/100 ml) active starter
- ½ cup (2¼ oz/60 g) organic spelt or rye flour

For the topping
- 3 tablespoons vegan soft cheese
- 1 teaspoon truffle oil
- ½ zucchini (courgette), thinly sliced
- 2 tablespoons pine nuts
- 10 sage leaves

Have you ever tried to barbecue a pizza? If not, you are in for a real treat. The outdoor grill (barbecue) is similar to a brick oven. If you don't happen to have an outdoor grill at home, you can use an oven and a pizza stone. Simply heat the oven (and the stone) to the highest possible temperature before putting in the pizza. I use a sourdough base, because it can be lighter for the digestion, but you can use normal yeast dough, if you prefer.

The easiest way to start baking with sourdough is to acquire a small batch of active sourdough starter from a friend or a good bakery. Transfer scant ½ cup (3½ fl oz/100 ml) starter to a bigger jar, feed with scant ½ cup (3½ fl oz/100 ml) water and ½ cup (2¼ oz/60 g) organic flour, stir, and lightly cover. Keep the jar in a warm place for 12 hours and then feed again with same amount of water and flour. Now the starter should be bubbly and ready to use. Store in the refrigerator and when you want to use the starter take it out the day before, feed, and stir.

Combine the sourdough starter and yogurt in a bowl. Add the spelt flour, baking powder, and salt and mix together until a soft, not sticky, dough forms. Add the olive oil and knead for a few minutes. If the dough sticks to your fingers, add a little more flour. Every sourdough starter has a slightly different moisture level so it is a good idea to have some extra flour on hand, if needed. Now put the dough into an airtight container and rest in a warm place for 2–4 hours. It should double in size and become airy.

Heat a pizza stone on your grill and divide the dough in half. Using a rolling pin, roll out 2 pizza crusts (bases) to a diameter of 9 inches (23 cm).

For the toppings, stir the cheese and oil together in a bowl, spread on the pizza crusts, and top with the zucchini (courgette), pine nuts, and sage leaves. Place your pizza on the hot stone (the easiest way is with a pizza paddle) and put in the grill. Bake for 5–8 minutes. If you don't have a pizza stone, grill the pizza in an aluminum tray instead.

Skyr with Coconut and Berry Jam

Serves 4

- ⅓ cup (3¼ oz/90 g) blueberry jam
- 1¼ cups (10 oz/300 g) vegetarian skyr, thick Greek yogurt, or vegan yogurt
- 4 tablespoons toasted flaked coconut
- ½ cup (2 oz/50 g) fresh blueberries
- a pinch of ground cardamom

Skyr is an Icelandic yogurt that has a very thick consistency. In this recipe you can use thick Greek yogurt or thick vegan yogurt instead of skyr, if you prefer.

Put 1 tablespoon blueberry jam into 4 small 4 fl oz (120 ml) jars, add 2 tablespoons of skyr, another 1 tablespoon blueberry jam, and 2 tablespoons skyr. Add a tablespoon of coconut flakes on top with some fresh blueberries and a sprinkling of ground cardamom. Enjoy straight from the jar.

Pink Lemonade

Serves 4

- generous 2 cups (17 fl oz/500 ml) sparkling mineral water
- 2 tablespoons Ginger Shot (see page 96)
- 1 tablespoon lime juice
- 1 tablespoon beet (beetroot) juice
- 1 tablespoon chia seeds
- ¼ teaspoon cayenne pepper
- 1 tablespoon coconut nectar, maple syrup, or a sweetener of your choice
- 10 mint leaves

Combine all the ingredients in a clean pitcher (jug) or a sterilized (see page 22) glass bottle.

Midday Lunch

One-Bowl Wonders

—

Fall Recipes and Activities

Hildur and I love to eat a delicious and satisfying meal in a bowl and it's always a little different than eating from a plate. When we crave a quick but nourishing meal, we make it in a bowl. In the bowl, try to make sure there is some protein, good-quality carbohydrates, vegetables, maybe some fruit, and always a really tasty dressing. The dressing is the keyword here, because a good dressing makes almost any food taste great.

There are three things to consider when making a dressing: the type of acid, the flavor, and the herbs. First, select your acid. Choose from: Lemon, lime, orange, grapefruit, apple cider vinegar, white wine vinegar, red wine vinegar, rice vinegar, or balsamic vinegar. Next, think about the taste you want: Miso, chipotle, chile, mustard, capers, garlic, ginger, tamari, spices, vegetarian Parmesan-style cheese or nutritional yeast, or sweet (honey, date, maple syrup, raisins, berries, fruits). Finally, select the herbs—if you like them: Cilantro (coriander), mint, parsley, dill, rosemary, chives, scallion (spring onion). I've included three dressings that make every bowl taste great (see page 122).

Enjoying a nourishing well-balanced meal in a bowl like this will make you feel satisfied and you won't need to snack throughout the day.

Mango and Herb Dressing

Makes 1½ cups (12 fl oz/350 ml)

- 1 cup (5 oz/150 g) mango cubes
- ¼ cup (2 fl oz/60 ml) lime juice
- ¼ cup (½ oz/10 g) cilantro (coriander)
- 2 tablespoons mint
- 2 tablespoons basil
- 2 tablespoons olive oil
- 1–2 dates, pitted
- 1 teaspoon salt
- ¾ teaspoons chopped chile

Put all the ingredients into a blender and blend well. Transfer to a clean glass jar and store in the refrigerator until ready to use.

Orange, Maple Syrup, and Mustard Dressing

Makes 1¼ cups (10 fl oz/300 ml)

- ½ cup (4 fl oz/120 ml) olive oil
- ¼ cup (2 fl oz/60 ml) balsamic vinegar
- ¼ cup (2 fl oz/60 ml) orange juice
- 2 tablespoons fresh basil
- 2 tablespoons mustard
- 2 tablespoons maple syrup or coconut nectar
- sea salt
- chopped chile, to taste

Put all the ingredients into a blender and blend well. Transfer to a clean glass jar and store in the refrigerator until ready to use.

Asian Cashew Dressing

Makes scant 2 cups (15 fl oz/450 ml)

- 1 cup (5 oz/150 g) cashew nuts
- ⅓ cup (2½ fl oz/75 ml) olive oil
- 1 tablespoon apple cider vinegar
- 3 tablespoons coconut nectar or maple syrup
- 3 tablespoons lemon juice
- 1 tablespoon onion powder
- 1 tablespoon vegan sambal oelek
- 1 clove garlic
- 1 teaspoon dill
- sea salt and freshly ground black pepper

Put the cashew nuts into a bowl, pour in enough water to cover, and soak for at least 2 hours. Drain and discard the soaking water.

Put the cashew nuts into a blender with the remaining ingredients, add ⅔ cup (5 fl oz/150 ml) water, and blend well. Transfer to a clean glass jar and store in the refrigerator until ready to use.

Quinoa and Amaranth Bowl with Black Beans and Kale

GF DF V

Serves 2

- 1 small or ½ large sweet potato, peeled and cut into cubes
- 1–2 teaspoons coconut oil
- 1 cup (4 oz/120 g) Brussels sprouts
- ½ cup (2¾ oz/75 g) quinoa
- ¼ cup (3⅓ oz/95 g) amaranth
- 5 cardamom pods
- 2 star anise
- 1 teaspoon red pepper (chili) flakes
- ½ teaspoon sea salt flakes
- 1½ cups (12 fl oz/350 ml) beet (beetroot) juice
- ½ cup (1¼ oz/35 g) chopped kale leaves (about 4 large leaves)
- ⅓ cup (2 oz/50 g) cooked black beans
- 3 figs, quartered
- 1 avocado, peeled, pitted and cut into cubes
- 10 almonds, dry-roasted in a pan
- salt and freshly ground black pepper

For the herb pesto
- ½ cup (2¾ oz/75 g) cashew nuts, toasted
- ¼ cup (¾ oz/20 g) cilantro (coriander)
- ¼ cup (⅙ oz/5 g) basil
- ¼ cup (⅙ oz/5 g) mint
- 2 tablespoons lemon juice
- 1 clove garlic
- 1–2 medjool dates, pitted (optional)
- 1 teaspoon red pepper (chili) flakes
- ½ teaspoon sea salt flakes
- ½ cup (4 fl oz/120 ml) olive oil

Preheat the oven to 345°F/170°C/Gas Mark 3–4 and line a baking sheet with parchment (baking) paper.

Put the sweet potato cubes onto the lined baking sheet, season with salt and pepper, add the coconut oil and 1–2 tablespoons water, then bake in the oven for 20–25 minutes. After 15 minutes add the Brussels sprouts to the baking sheet.

Put the quinoa, amaranth, cardamom pods, star anise, red pepper (chili) flakes, and sea salt into a saucepan. Pour in the beet (beetroot) juice and bring to a boil. Reduce the heat and simmer for 18–20 minutes, or until cooked. Turn off the heat, cover with a lid, and let stand for 5 minutes.

For the herb pesto, put all the ingredients into a blender and blend until smooth. Transfer to a clean glass jar or a bowl, cover, and set aside.

To serve, put the quinoa and amaranth in the bottom of a bowl and add the remaining ingredients. Finish with a spoonful of the herb pesto.

Tip: It is easier to buy canned black beans to use in this recipe but if you have time, it is more economical to boil them yourself. Soak the dried black beans in a bowl of water overnight. The next day, drain, rinse, put into a saucepan, and cover with fresh water. Bring to a boil over high heat and boil for about 10 minutes, skimming off any foam with a slotted spoon. Reduce the heat and simmer for about 1 hour, or until tender. Drain and set aside.

Baked Beet Bowl

Serves 2

- 1 tablespoon fennel seeds
- 3 beets (beetroots), peeled and cut into cubes
- 1 teaspoon sea salt flakes
- 1 tablespoon coconut oil
- ½ head broccoli, cut into florets
- 2–3 kale leaves, stems (stalks) removed and leaves chopped
- 2 tablespoons olive oil
- 2 tablespoons lemon juice
- 2 teaspoons grated fresh ginger root
- 1 teaspoon toasted sesame oil
- 1 avocado, peeled, pitted, and cut into cubes
- 2 oz (50 g) soft goat cheese, soft vegan cheese, or tofu, crumbled
- ½ cup (2 oz/50 g) walnuts, toasted
- 3 kumquats, thinly sliced
- 2 tablespoons hemp seeds

For the millet
- ⅓ cup (2¼ oz/65 g) millet
- 1 teaspoon fennel seeds
- ¼ teaspoon sea salt flakes
- 1 tablespoon olive oil

To finish
- olive oil
- balsamic vinegar
- sea salt flakes

Start by cooking the millet. Put the millet and fennel seeds into a saucepan over medium heat and dry-roast for 5 minutes, or until golden. Be careful not to let it burn. Pour in ⅔ cup (5 fl oz/150 ml) water, then add the sea salt flakes and olive oil, stir, and bring to a boil. Reduce the heat and simmer for about 15 minutes, or until cooked. Turn off the heat, cover the pan, and let stand for about 10 minutes. Using 2 forks, fluff up the millet and set aside.

Meanwhile, preheat the oven to 350°F/180°C/Gas Mark 4.

Put the fennel seeds into a small bowl and add 1 tablespoon water.

Put the beet (beetroot) cubes on a nonstick baking sheet, sprinkle with the sea salt and fennel seeds mixed with water, and dot with the coconut oil. Bake in the oven for about 30 minutes.

Put the broccoli and kale in a bowl. Whisk the olive oil, lemon juice, grated ginger, and toasted sesame oil together in a small bowl, then pour the mixture over the broccoli and kale. Using your hands, massage it into the kale and broccoli for 2–3 minutes, making sure they are well coated.

Put the cooked millet into a bowl, add the beets, broccoli, kale, and the remaining ingredients. To finish, sprinkle with a little olive oil, balsamic vinegar, and sea salt flakes. Enjoy.

Tip: If you are vegan or dairy free, then add tofu or vegan cheese instead of the goat cheese.

Lentil Salad with Brussels Sprouts and Spicy Pecans

Serves 4–6

- 1 eggplant (aubergine), cut into quarters lengthwise, then into ¾ inch (2 cm) pieces
- 7 oz (200 g) Brussels sprouts, cut in half
- 3 tablespoons olive oil
- 5 cloves garlic, chopped
- 1 teaspoon paprika
- 1 teaspoon sea salt flakes
- 1 mango, peeled, seeded, and cut into cubes
- 2 avocados, peeled, pitted and cut into cubes
- ⅓ cup (1½ oz/45 g) dried mulberries
- 10 raspberries
- 1 handful of fresh herbs, such as cilantro (coriander), basil, mint, or parsley), finely chopped (use 2 varieties)
- freshly ground black pepper
- sprouts, to garnish (optional)

For the French green lentils
- ¾ cup (2¾ oz/75 g) French green (Puy) lentils (see tip, below)
- 1 sprig rosemary
- 2 cloves garlic
- 1 inch (2.5 cm) piece fresh red chile
- sea salt flakes
- ¼ teaspoon baking powder

For the spicy pecans
- ⅓ cup (2 oz/50 g) pecans
- 1 tablespoon coconut nectar or maple syrup
- 1 teaspoon red pepper (chili) flakes
- pinch of sea salt

For the dressing
- ¼ cup (2 fl oz/60 ml) olive oil
- 1 teaspoon horseradish
- 1 tablespoon capers
- juice of 1 orange
- 1 medjool date, pitted and chopped
- a pinch of sea salt flakes

Beans and lentils are a great source of plant-based protein. They are also inexpensive and easy to use, which makes them perfect for salads. For this delicious salad we have used french green (Puy) lentils. You don't need to soak them before cooking but we always do because we find them easier to digest.

Preheat the oven to 400°F/200°C/Gas Mark 6.

Start by cooking the lentils. Put the lentils into a saucepan with the rest of the ingredients, pour in 2 cups (16 fl oz/475 ml) boiling water, and bring to a boil over high heat. Reduce the heat and simmer for about 20 minutes. Turn the heat off and let stand for about 5 minutes, then strain the lentils to remove any excess liquid. Set aside.

Line a baking sheet with parchment (baking) paper. Put the eggplant (aubergine) and Brussels sprouts onto the prepared sheet and sprinkle with the olive oil, chopped garlic, paprika, the salt, and freshly ground black pepper. Bake in the oven for 15 minutes.

Meanwhile, make the spicy pecans. Put the nuts into a saucepan, add the coconut nectar or maple syrup, red pepper (chili) flakes, and salt and toast over medium heat for 5–7 minutes, making sure it doesn't burn. Remove from the heat and set aside.

To make the dressing, put all the ingredients into a blender and blend until smooth. Alternatively, put everything in a clean jar, put the lid on, and shake together until combined.

To serve, put everything into a large serving bowl, mix well, and arrange beautifully. Pour over the dressing, garnish with sprouts, if using, and enjoy.

Tip: If you would like to soak the lentils before using, then put them into a bowl, pour in enough water to cover, and soak for 1–2 hours. Drain and discard the soaking water.

Midday/Lunch/One-Bowl Wonders

Thai Slaw

Serves 4–6 as a side dish

- ½ small head (about 9 oz/250 g) red cabbage, cut into thin strips
- 9 oz (250 g) pineapple, peeled, cored, and cut into small pieces
- 2 carrots, very thinly sliced using a vegetable peeler
- 1 red bell pepper, cut into thin strips
- 1 celery, thinly sliced
- 2–3 scallions (spring onions), cut into thin strips
- 1 handful of sprouts
- 1 handful of cilantro (coriander), chopped
- ¼ handful of mint, chopped
- ¼ handful of basil, chopped
- 1 tablespoon black sesame seeds

For the dressing
- ½ cup (4 fl oz/120 g) almond butter
- ¼ cup (2 fl oz/60 ml) lime juice
- 1 clove garlic
- 1 kaffir lime leave
- ½ teaspoon curry powder
- ½ teaspoon sea salt flakes
- ¼ teaspoon ground cumin
- a pinch of cayenne pepper
- 2 tablespoons chopped cilantro (coriander)

This recipe is extra flavorful if you thinly slice every ingredient so they absorb the dressing. A mandoline is the perfect tool for slicing the vegetables extremely thinly, but don't worry if you don't have one; you can use a vegetable peeler instead. When we have time, we massage the cabbage and carrots slices with some lemon juice and olive oil before assembling the slaw. For a nut-free version, use tahini instead of almond butter.

For the dressing, put all the ingredients, except the cilantro (coriander), into a blender with ½ cup (4 fl oz/120 ml) water and blend until smooth. Add the cilantro and blend for another a few minutes. Set aside.

Put all the vegetables and herbs into a bowl and mix together well. Pour the dressing over the salad and give it a little massage with your hands so everything is well coated. Serve.

Beautiful Raw Root Salad

Serves 4–6

- 11 oz (300 g) red cabbage,
  cut into thin strips
- 2 carrots, cut into thin round slices
- 1 zucchini (courgette), cut into
  thin round slices
- 1 yellow beet (beetroot), cut into
  thin round slices
- 1 striped or red beet (beetroot),
  cut into thin round slices
- 5 radishes, cut into thin slices
- 1 pear, cut in half, cored and cut
  into thin slices
- seeds of 1 pomegranate
- ⅓ cup (2 oz/50 g) pistachios
- 10 dried Incan golden berries
- 4 tablespoons green herbs, such
  as cilantro (coriander), mint,
  basil, and parsley, finely chopped

For the dressing
- scant ¼ cup (1¾ fl oz/50 ml)
  walnut or olive oil
- 3 tablespoons lemon juice
- 3 tablespoons mandarin juice
  or orange juice
- 1 tablespoon rice vinegar
  (or your favorite vinegar)
- 1 teaspoon ras-el-hanout spice
- 1 teaspoon onion powder
- ½ teaspoon sea salt

When we look at beautiful foods, our digestive system starts to wake up, so we might argue that we start eating with our eyes—this salad is definitely a feast for the eyes. Hildur and I like to slice the roots very thinly, preferably using a mandoline or a vegetable peeler. The vegetables are even tastier and softer if they are marinated in the dressing for a while.

To make the dressing, put all the ingredients into a clean jar, put the lid on, and shake together. Set aside.

Put all the prepared vegetables into a bowl, pour over the dressing, then using your fingers, massage the dressing into the vegetables. Let marinate for 15–20 minutes.

When ready to eat, put the vegetables into a serving bowl, add the remaining ingredients, toss together, and enjoy.

Fragrances of Asia in a Soup with Kelp Noodles

Serves 3–4

For the paste
- 1 teaspoon coriander seeds
- 1 oz (25 g) piece fresh ginger root, peeled
- ⅛ oz (5 g) piece fresh galangal, peeled
- 5 kaffir lime leaves
- 2 red chiles, seeded
- 2 cloves garlic
- 1 stalk lemongrass, trimmed, outer layers removed, and chopped
- 1 teaspoon tamarind paste
- 10 cilantro (coriander) sprigs
- 3 tablespoons coconut oil
- 1 teaspoon toasted sesame oil

For the soup
- 9 oz (250 g) kelp noodles
- 11 oz (300 g) plum tomatoes, coarsely chopped
- 2 red bell peppers, cored and diced
- 1 x 14 fl oz (400 ml) can coconut milk
- 1⅔ cups (14 fl oz/400 ml) vegetable broth (stock)
- 1 tablespoon tamari

For the toppings
- 1 tablespoon chopped mint
- 1 tablespoon chopped cilantro (coriander)
- 1 tablespoon Thai basil
- 1 inch (2.5 cm) piece red chile, thinly sliced
- 1 scallion (spring onion), thinly sliced
- 1 small carrot, very finely sliced
- Kale Chips (see page 114),
- 2 tablespoons toasted flaked coconut
- lime wedges, quartered

Put the kelp noodles for the soup into a bowl, pour in enough water to cover, and soak for 20 minutes. Drain, discard the soaking water, and pat the kelp dry with paper towels. Set aside.

For the paste, toast the coriander seeds in a dry pan over low heat for 2–3 minutes. Transfer to a spice grinder or grind in a morter with a pestle. Put into a food processor with all the other paste ingredients and blend until smooth.

Put the paste into a saucepan and cook over medium heat for 1 minute, or until it smells aromatic. Add the tomatoes and bell peppers and cook for 5 minutes. Add the coconut milk, broth (stock), and tamari and bring to a boil. Reduce the heat and simmer for 4 minutes.

Divide the kelp noodles among 4 soup bowls. Pour the soup over the noodles, garnish with the toppings, and squeeze the lime, if using, into the soup. Enjoy.

Tip: If you can't find galangal, you can use some more ginger instead. The toppings add crunch to the soup as well as flavor. Use the ones you like.

Icelandic Kimchi

Makes about 2 ¼ lb (1 kg)

- ½ small head (about 7 oz/200 g) red cabbage, very thinly sliced
- 1 red bell pepper, seeded and cut into thin strips
- 4 red radishes, very thinly sliced
- 2 carrots, cut into very thin strips
- ½ head cauliflower, cut into bite-size pieces
- 3 tablespoons sea salt flakes

For the vinegar blend
- 1 cup (8 fl oz/250 ml) apple cider vinegar
- 1 tablespoon tamari
- 1 tablespoon coconut palm sugar
- 2 tablespoons Ginger Shot (see page 96)
- 6 cloves garlic
- 3 tablespoons chili paste

We were brought up with fermented vegetables as a side dish with almost every meal. In addition to enriching the meal with flavor, it is also very nutritious and can aid digestion. Most food cultures have their own recipe for fermented vegetables. In Korea, kimchi is very traditional, so we have made our own version using vegetables that grow in our garden and greenhouse. We have also made it less spicy.

Put all the vegetables into a large bowl, sprinkle the sea salt flakes on top, and toss together. Cover with a clean dish cloth and let stand at a room temperature for 4–6 hours, stirring once in a while.

Rinse the salt off the vegetables under cold water and pat dry with paper towels or a clean dish cloth. Put the vegetables into a clean bowl.

Put all the ingredients for the vinegar blend into a sterilized (see page 22) glass jar, put the lid on, and shake until combined. Pour the vinegar blend over the vegetables, cover, and let marinate at room temperature for 2–4 hours or overnight. You can let them marinate for up to 2–3 days, if you like. The longer they marinate the stronger the taste will be. Pack the marinated vegetables into sterilized jars and store in the refrigerator or in a cool place. This will keep for up to 2 weeks in the refrigerator.

Beet and Sweet Potato Soup

Serves 4

- 1 tablespoon olive oil
- 1 onion, thinly sliced
- 2 teaspoons ground cumin
- ¾ teaspoon ground turmeric
- ½–1 teaspoon salt
- ¼ teaspoon cayenne pepper
- 3 beets (beetroots), peeled and cut into small pieces
- 1 sweet potato, peeled and cut into small pieces
- 1 x 14 oz (400 g) can coconut milk

To garnish
- cold-pressed olive oil, to drizzle
- 4 tablespoons Sour Cashew Cream (see page 170), optional
- 4 tablespoons toasted flaked coconut (optional)
- 2 tablespoons finely chopped parsley (optional)

Preparing beets (beetroot) without the somewhat overpowering earthy flavor can be tricky. The spices we use for this soup are magic: When the cumin and turmeric blend with the beets and sweet potato it's delicious. We include it as part of our simple two-day cleasing menu but thinned down with a little more water (see page 70).

Heat the oil in a saucepan over low heat, add the onion, and cook for 10 minutes, or until soft. Don't let the onion burn. Season with the spices and add the remaining ingredients. Pour in 2½ cups (20 fl oz/ 600 ml water), bring to a boil, and boil over medium heat for 45–60 minutes, or until the beets are soft.

Put the soup into a blender and blend until smooth. Pour into 4 bowls and drizzle each serving with olive oil. Alternatively, top with sour cashew cream, toasted coconut, and parsley.

Young Coconut Soup

Serve 3–4

For the soup
- 2 young coconuts, use both the coconut water and coconut meat, or you can use 2 x 14 oz (400 g) cans coconut milk
- 2 kaffir lime leaves
- 4-inch (10-cm) stalk lemongrass, outer layer removed, and chopped
- 2 cloves garlic
- 1 tablespoon very finely chopped fresh ginger root
- 1 teaspoon very finely chopped fresh galangal (optional)
- 1 whole lime, peeled
- 1 teaspoon sea salt flakes
- 1 teaspoon Thai curry paste
- a pinch of cayenne pepper

To garnish
- 2 carrots, very finely sliced
- 2 scallions (spring onions), very thinly sliced
- 1 handful of snow peas (mangetout), thinly sliced
- 1 avocado, peeled, pitted, and cut into cubes
- ½ red bell pepper, cut into cubes
- finely chopped fresh herbs, such as mint, cilantro (coriander), and basil

Put all the ingredients for the soup into a blender and blend until smooth. Pour the soup into serving bowls and top with a handful of the vegetable and herb garnishes.

Tip: You can use store-bought curry paste or you can use the one from the Fragrances of Asia in a Soup recipe on page 134.

Everything from the Garden Soup

Serves 4

- 2 tablespoons olive oil
- 7 oz (200 g) leeks, chopped
- 2 cloves garlic
- ½ teaspoon smoked paprika
- 2 tablespoons dried soup herbs or 1 bouillon (stock) cube
- ½ cup (3½ oz/100 g) barley
- 2 carrots, chopped
- 7 oz (200 g) celeriac, diced
- 7 oz (200 g) potato, diced
- 7 oz (200 g) turnip, diced
- ½ small head (about 7 oz/200 g) cabbage, chopped
- 4 tomatoes, cut into quarters
- 2 rosemary sprigs
- 3 cups (25 fl oz/750 ml) vegetable broth (stock)
- cilantro (coriander) and flat-leaf parsley, for sprinkling
- Wild Sorrel Pesto (see page 144), to serve (optional)

One of the big pleasures of fall (autumn) is the aroma of home-grown vegetables boiling in a big pot for a nourishing soup. After getting rid of many weeds and picking off the slugs and watering the vegetables with devotion, it is wonderful to harvest everything that has grown. If we haven't managed to grow any vegetables that year, we can still appreciate the huge selection of fresh newly picked produce at the market.

If you are not following a nut-free diet and you have some wild sorrel pesto, you can serve that with this soup, too.

Heat the olive oil in a large heavy stockpot over medium heat. Once the oil is hot, add the leek and garlic and cook for 2–3 minutes, until they begin to soften. Add the smoked paprika, soup herbs, and barley and continue to cook for 4 minutes, stirring occasionally. Now add the carrot, celeriac, potato, turnip, cabbage, tomatoes, and rosemary sprigs and cook for another 2–3 minutes. Pour in the broth (stock) and cook for about 25 minutes, or until the vegetables are tender.

Serve the soup in bowls, sprinkled with cilantro (coriander) and flat-leaf parsley over each serving.

Wild Sorrel Pesto

Makes ¾ cup (6 fl oz/175 ml)

- 2 cups (2 oz/50 g) wild sorrel
  (or basil if sorrel doesn't
  grow in your area)
- scant ¼ cup (1 oz/30 g)
  cashew nuts, dry roasted
- 1 clove garlic
- ½–1 teaspoon sea salt
- 1 teaspoon lemon juice
- ⅓ cup–scant ½ cup
  (2½–3½ fl oz/75–100 ml)
  olive oil

Sorrel is a leafy grass that grows wild in Iceland. It looks similar to spinach but tastes amazing. It has a sweet and sour taste and children love it. I have fond memories of picking wild sorrel and putting it straight into my mouth while playing outside when I was a child. You can use it as a sauce for pasta or as a topping for crackers.

Put all the ingredients, except the olive oil, into a food processor and blend well. Alternatively, put everything, except the olive oil, into a mortar and mash with the pestle. Transfer to a bowl and stir in the olive oil. Store in the refrigerator for up to 10 days in an airtight container.

Fall Recipes and Activities

Picking Wild Berries

Late summer and early fall (autumn) many Icelanders travel to the countryside to pick crowberries (similar to blackberries) and blueberries that grow wild on the hillsides around the country. In the following weeks, the whole nation is occupied with making crowberry sap, blueberry jam and pies, and freezing wild berries for the winter. It is part of Icelandic tradition, and everyone gets to spend time outdoors with their family and friends. I have fond memories of coming home tired but happy, sporting a purple tongue, lungs full of oxygen, and carrying full jars of wild berries. What could be better?

Wild Berry Jam

Makes 5 cups (40 fl oz/1.2 liters)

- 4 cups (1 lb 5 oz/600 g) blueberries
- ⅓ cup (1½ oz/50 g) dried mulberries or medjool dates
- 2–4 tablespoons coconut palm sugar
- 3 tablespoons lemon juice
- 2-inch (5-cm) piece of fresh ginger root, peeled
- 1–2 teaspoons vanilla powder
- 1 teaspoon ground cinnamon
- 1 teaspoon ground turmeric
- ¼ teaspoon cayenne pepper
- a pinch of sea salt flakes
- 2 tablespoons ground chia seeds

Feel free to use your favorite sweetener in this recipe. You can use dates instead of coconut palm sugar, or add more mulberries. Hildur and I like to make a small batch each time, so we use less sugar.

Put all the ingredients, except the chia seeds, into a saucepan. Bring to a boil, stirring constantly. Let it boil for 5 minutes, then add the chia seeds, reduce the heat, and simmer for 2–4 minutes, until it begins to thicken. Stir constantly to prevent the jam from burning. Pour the jam into sterilized (see page 22) 10 oz (300 ml) jars and let cool. Seal with lids and store in the refrigerator.

Wild Berry Pie

Serves 8

- ½ cup (4 fl oz/120 ml) coconut oil, plus extra to grease
- generous ¾ cup (3½ oz/100 g) spelt flour or gluten-free flour blend
- generous 1 cup (4¾ oz/140 g) gluten-free rolled oats
- ¾ cup (3 oz/80 g) almond flour
- scant ½ cup (3¼ oz/90 g) coconut palm sugar
- 1 teaspoon ground cinnamon
- ½ teaspoon sea salt flakes
- ¾ cup (4 oz/120 g) frozen blueberries
- scant ⅓ cup (3½ oz/100 g) blueberry jam

Blueberries are very nutritious and have lots of health benefits. They contain pigments called anthocyanins, which give them their purple color. These pigments are antioxidants and are thought to protect the body from heart disease as well as improve memory.

Preheat the oven to 375°F/190°C/Gas Mark 5 and lightly grease 9-inch (23-cm) pie pan.

Put the spelt flour, oats, almond flour, coconut palm sugar, cinnamon, and salt flakes into a large bowl and mix together. Add the coconut oil and knead until it becomes sticky and crumbly.

Press scant 3 cups (15 oz/420 g) of the crumbly mixture into the prepared pie pan with your fingertips to form a crust. Spread the blueberry jam over the crust, pour the frozen blueberries over the jam, and finish by spreading the rest of the crumbly mixture over the blueberries. Bake for 25 minutes, or until browned on top. Cool on a wire rack.

Fermented Carrots with Spices (Family Recipe)

   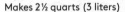

Makes 2½ quarts (3 liters)

- 4½ lb (2 kg) carrots, grated
- 1 lb 2 oz (500 g) turnips, grated
- 7 oz (200 g) white onions, chopped
- 2 oz (50 g) scallions (spring onions), chopped
- 1 green chile, chopped
- 10 cloves garlic
- scant ¼ cup (1 oz/25 g) sea salt flakes
- ½ cup (1 oz/25 g) tarragon, chopped
- ⅓ cup (1 oz/25 g) parsley, chopped
- 1 teaspoon mustard seeds
- 2 bay leaves
- 2 cloves
- scant ¼ cup (1¾ fl oz/50 ml) sauerkraut juice or juice from a former batch
- 2–3 pieces of white cabbage leaves

Grandma Hildur and Grandpa Eiríkur used to grow more vegetables than the family could use. As a result they started experimenting with fermenting so that nothing would be wasted. A successful fermentation extends the shelf life of the produce and changes the flavor, texture, and nutritional value of the food. In a way, we can compare fermentation to a sort of predigestion, where microorganisms begin the breakdown. It is a part of the cycle of nature and, if left undisturbed, would end in total decomposition into soil. This wonderful recipe for fermented carrots is the one Grandma Hildur has developed over the years and every year she makes a big batch of them for the whole family to enjoy. For best results, use organic carrots and you will need a 2½ quart (3 liter) jar.

In a sterilized (see page 22) wide-mouthed 2½-quart (3-liter) jar, add all the vegetables in layers, sprinkling sea salt flakes, herbs, and spices between the layers. Using a thick wooden stick, tamp down the vegetables. This helps to release the fluid and get rid of the air in the jar. After each layer, pour a tablespoon or so of the sauerkraut juice over the vegetables, this helps with the fermentation. When the jar is almost full, the juice should cover the vegetables. If not, add some boiled cooled water and then cover the top with 2–3 cabbage leaves. Cover the jar with a tight-fitting lid and a rubber band.

Store in a dark room at 64–68°F/18–20°C for the first 10 days, then transfer to the refrigerator or other cold storage and keep for 6–8 weeks. We like to put the fermented carrots into smaller jars, because they are easier to store. They keep for a few months in a cool place. We eat these with everything as a condiment.

Fermented Beet (Family Recipe)

Makes 2½ quarts (3-liters)

- 1 tablespoon good-quality salt
- 2¼ lb (1 kg) beets (beetroots), finely grated
- 4 green apples, cored and finely grated
- ½ cup (4 fl oz/120 ml) juice from former batch or a good-quality culture
- 2 kaffir lime leaves
- 1 stalk lemongrass
- 1 tablespoon grated fresh ginger root
- 1 teaspoon caraway seeds
- 1 teaspoon mint
- ½ teaspoon ground turmeric
- ¼ teaspoon shatavari
- ¼ teaspoon holy basil
- cabbage or collard leaf, rolled up

For best results, use organic beets (beetroot) and you will need a 2½-quart (3-liter) jar with a rubber lip.

Bring 2½ cups (20 fl oz/600 ml) water to a boil then cool it to room temperature. Add the salt, stir, and let it dissolve.

In a sterilized (see page 22) wide-mouthed 2½-quart (3-liter) jar, add the grated vegetables, apples, herbs, spices, and salt mixture. Pack the vegetables down tightly. Pour in some water to cover the vegetables (make sure they are not exposed to air), then put a rolled up cabbage leaf or a collard leaf on the top to keep the vegetables well packed. Screw on the lid tightly.

Store in a dark room at 64–68°F/18–20°C for the first 10 days, then transfer to the refrigerator or other cold storage and keep for 2 weeks. After 2 weeks, strain the juice from the vegetables and apples and transfer them to smaller sterilized jars and store in the refrigerator or another cold place. Pour the strained juice into a sterilized bottle. Both the fermented vegetables and the juice keep for months in the refrigerator or in a cool storage. We love to sip a little of the juice first thing in the morning on an empty stomach. It's a great enery booster, because it helps transport oxygen and nutrients to various parts of the body.

Guide For Storing Fresh Herbs

Fresh herbs take meals to another level. If you grow herbs in your backyard, garden, balcony, or kitchen window, you know how wonderful it is to be able to reach for some fresh herbs when you need them. In late fall (autumn), it gets harder to maintain most herbs, even inside, at least here up in the North, where the days get shorter and shorter and sunlight is rare. If we haven't managed to use all our herbs as we go during the summer, now is the time to harvest and store them for winter. Pesto (see page 144) is a delicious way to use up large amounts of fresh herbs, but here are a few more tips for storing herbs.

1. Cut herbs:
   These can be kept fresh for a few days in the same way as a flower bouquet in a vase with water. Place a wet paper towel around the stems (stalks) and store in a sealed plastic bag, or a jar with a lid, in the refrigerator for a few days.

2. Dry:
   Some herbs, especially ones with coarse stems (stalks), such as rosemary and thyme, are well suited to drying. Hang the stems upside down for 2 weeks to dry whole, or take the leaves or needles from the stems and lay flat on a dry cloth for 2 weeks. Dried herbs can be stored in airtight containers for 4–6 months.

3. Freeze:
   Freezing is a good way to store many herbs. Before you pick a method, you need to decide what you would like to use the herbs for.

Ice cubes:
Herbs that we would like to use in hot or cold drinks are perfect for freezing in water. Place whole leaves, chopped up herbs, or edible flowers in an ice-cube tray and fill up with water. The ice cubes will turn out beautiful and will make cold drinks much more festive. The ice cubes can also be defrosted and used in herbal tea. This is a great idea for mint, both in mojitos and tea. Once frozen, the ice cubes can be stored in small freezer bags for 6 months. Remember to label the bag so you know what's inside.

Oil cubes:
Basil, cilantro (coriander), mint, rosemary needles, thyme leaves, dill, and parsley can be chopped in a food processor with extra virgin olive oil. Freeze the herb-oil mixture in small bags or in ice-cube trays, then when frozen, transfer to marked bags. These cubes are perfect for sauces, soups, and stews during the winter. They can also be defrosted and used for making pesto or added to hummus. They keep well in the freezer for up to 4–5 months.

Homemade Seed Bread

Makes 2 loaves

- coconut oil, to grease
- 2 cups (7 oz/200 g) gluten-free rolled oats
- 4 cups (10 oz/550 g) seed blend
- 1 cup (5 oz/150 g) chopped pecans
- ¾ cup (2¼ oz/60 g) psyllium husks
- ½ cup (3 oz/80 g) ground chia seeds
- 1–2 teaspoons sea salt flakes
- ¼ cup (2 fl oz/60 ml) olive oil
- 2 tablespoons coconut nectar or maple syrup

We love to use a mixture of seeds in this bread: Sunflower, pumpkin, hemp, and flaxseeds.

Preheat the oven to 350°F/180°C/Gas Mark 4 and grease 2 8 x 4 x 2½-inch/20 x 10 x 6-cm loaf pans.

Combine all the dry ingredients together in a large bowl and mix together.

In another bowl, combine the olive oil, 3 cups (25 fl oz/750 ml) water, and coconut nectar. Add this to the dry ingredients and blend together until the dough is the consistency of thick oatmeal (porridge). Put the dough into the prepared loaf pans, cover with a clean dish towel, and let rest at room temperature for 30–60 minutes before baking.

Bake in the oven for 30 minutes, then remove the bread from the pans, put them onto a nonstick baking sheet, and bake for another 30–35 minutes, or until golden brown. This bread needs to cool completely before slicing and keeps for 5–7 days in the refrigerator. It also bread freezes well. Slice it before freezing so that it's easier to put in the toaster when hungry.

Tip: If you are allergic to nuts, omit the pecans and add the same amount of blended seeds.

Homemade Butter

Makes 1 cup (8 oz/225 g)

- 2 cups (16 fl oz/475 ml) heavy (double) cream
- 1½ teaspoons salt (optional)
- 2 tablespoons chopped cilantro (coriander), optional
- 2 teaspoons lime juice (optional)
- 1 teaspoon lime zest
- ¼ teaspoon cayenne pepper
- 1 teaspoon salt
- Homemade Seed Bread (see above), to serve

Pour the cream into a food processor and process for 8–10 minutes, or until the butter separates. Strain off the liquid into a bowl. At this point you can either add 1½ teaspoons salt for a plain butter or some spices. I love to add cilantro (coriander) and lime. Stir in the chopped cilantro, lime juice, lime zest, cayenne pepper, and salt. Store in the refrigerator until you are ready to use.

Serve with some homemade seed bread.

Evening

Dinner

A Little More Time

—

Winter Recipes and Activities

Food tastes so much better when we make time to enjoy it. In our busy modern lives we are too rushed to think about preparing good food at home. However, it is important to make time to prepare food from scratch, at least some of the time, because we have better control over what type of foods we are eating and can make sensible decisions on choosing the ingredients ourselves. The best part is that it really doesn't have to be time consuming at all. Often it takes less time to make a delicious meal from scratch than to order a takeout (takeaway) or wait for a home delivery.

But to make it work, it pays to be organized and think ahead. It is good to keep a small well-stocked pantry of necessities and ingredients that allows you to whip up a quick meal in minutes. Hildur and I like to make our own variety of spice blends to have at hand, because we find that spices are essential to the food we make and can transform simple produce into a festive meal without too much fuss.

If you have some spare time, it's a good idea to prepare for the coming week, for example, plan a menu or make batches of dressings, pesto, baked vegetables, beans, and other useful things so you can quickly make a meal when you are rushed off your feet. As a small contrast to our modern fast food culture, let's make time to make, eat, and enjoy.

Rainbow Pasta with Pesto

Serves 3–4

- 1 rutabaga (swede)
- 1–2 carrots
- 1 beet (beetroot)
- 1 small zucchini (courgette)
- 2 tablespoons lemon juice
- 1 tablespoon olive oil

For the green pesto
- ½ cup (2¾ oz/75 g) cashew nuts
- 1 handful of basil
- 2–3 kale leaves, stems (stalks) removed
- 1–2 tablespoons nutritional yeast flakes
- 1 large clove garlic
- ¼–½ teaspoon sea salt flakes
- ¼–½ teaspoon cold-pressed olive oil

For the pesto, put the cashew nuts into a bowl, pour in enough water to cover, and soak for about 2 hours. Drain and discard the soaking water.

Put the cashew nuts into a food processor with the remaining ingredients, except the olive oil, and blend. The texture of the pesto should be chunky. Transfer the pesto to a bowl and add the olive oil. Stir gently to mix together. Spoon into a clean glass jar and set aside.

Peel the rutabaga (swede), carrots, and beet (beetroot) and use a julienne peeler or spiralizer to shred the vegetables into spaghetti-like strips.

Put your vegetable spaghetti into a bowl and add the lemon juice and olive oil. Stir together, then cover with plastic wrap (clingfilm) and leave for 15–25 minutes to let the "spaghetti" soften. Serve with the green pesto.

Lasagna

Serves 4

- 1 zucchini (courgette)
- 2 avocadoes, peeled, pitted, and cut into slices

For the Brazil nut cheese
- ½ cup (2¾ oz/75 g) Brazil nuts
- ¼ cup (1½ oz/40 g) cashew nuts
- 2 tablespoons lemon juice
- 2–3 tablespoons nutritional yeast flakes
- 1 teaspoon probiotic powder
- 1 teaspoon onion powder
- ½ teaspoon sea salt
- freshly ground black pepper

For the green pesto
- ½ cup (2¾ oz/75 g) cashew nuts
- 1 handful of basil
- 1 handful of arugula (rocket)
- 1–2 tablespoons nutritional yeast flakes
- 1 large clove garlic
- ¼–½ teaspoon sea salt flakes
- ¼–½ teaspoon cold-pressed olive oil

For the marinade
- 2 tablespoons lemon juice
- 1 tablespoons olive oil
- ½ teaspoon garlic powder
- ½ teaspoon dried oregano

For the red pesto
- 1¼ cups (4 oz/125 g) sun-dried tomatoes in oil, drained
- 2 plum tomatoes, pitted
- ½ red bell pepper, cored and seeded
- 1 clove garlic
- 2 dates, pitted and finely chopped
- 1 teaspoon dried oregano
- a pinch of sea salt

For the Brazil nut cheese, put the Brazil nuts and cashew nuts into in a bowl, pour in enough water to cover, and soak for 2–4 hours. Drain and discard the soaking water. Set aside.

For the green pesto, put the cashew nuts into a bowl, pour in enough water to cover, and soak for 2 hours. Drain and discard the soaking water. Set aside.

For the marinade, put all the ingredients into a bowl and mix together. Set aside.

Use a mandoline or a cheese slicer to cut the zucchini (courgettes) into long, thin slices. Put them into a bowl with the marinade, stir to coat the zucchini (courgette) in the marinade, cover with plastic wrap (clingfilm), and let stand while you make the pesto and cheese.

For the green pesto, put the cashew nuts into a food processor with the remaining ingredients, except the olive oil, and blend. The texture of the pesto should be chunky. Transfer the pesto to a bowl and add the olive oil. Stir gently to mix together. Set aside.

To make the red pesto, put all the ingredients into a food processor and blend until chunky. Add a little salt, if needed, then transfer to a bowl and set aside.

To make the Brazil nut cheese, put the drained Brazil nuts into a food processor with all the remaining ingredients. Season with pepper, add 2–3 tablespoons water, and blend until smooth. Transfer to a bowl and set aside.

To assemble the lasagna, arrange a layer of zucchini (courgette) in a shallow dish, add a layer of green pesto on top, followed by a layer of the nut cheese. Add another layer of zucchini, then a layer of the red pesto and a layer of sliced avocado. Repeat until all the ingredients are used up, finishing with the nut cheese. Alternatively, you can assemble individual servings on each of 4 plates.

Falafel with Sesame Seed Sauce

Serves 4

For the falafel
- 1½ cups (8 oz/225 g) almonds
- 1½ cups (5 oz/150 g) walnuts
- ½ cup (2½ oz/70 g) sesame seed paste (tahini)
- ¼ cup (1½ oz/40 g) raisins
- ½ cup (½ oz/15 g) parsley
- ½ cup (½ oz/15 g) cilantro (coriander), plus extra to garnish
- 2 cloves garlic
- 1 tablespoon ground coriander
- 1 tablespoon ground cumin
- 2 tablespoons coconut oil
- 2 tablespoons lemon juice
- 2 teaspoons salt
- ½ teaspoon ground black pepper

For the sauce
- 3 tablespoons lemon juice
- ⅓ cup (2½ fl oz/75 ml) orange juice
- ⅔ cup (3¼ oz/90 g) sesame seed paste (tahini)
- 3 cloves garlic, crushed
- ½ teaspoon Himalayan salt or sea salt
- 2 tablespoons cilantro (coriander)
- 1 tablespoon parsley
- 1 teaspoon curry powder
- ½ teaspoon ground cumin
- 2 dates, pitted (optional)

To serve
- 10 cooked wraps or romaine lettuce leaves
- Fermented Carrots with Spices (see page 155)

Do not let the long list of ingredients discourage you—this is really a very simple recipe. Falafel is exceptionally good in a cooked wrap or romaine lettuce with some homemade fermented carrots, sesame seed sauce, and fresh vegetables, such as ripe tomatoes, onions, and cucumber. The sauce is great for falafel and salad.

To make the falafel, put all the ingredients into a food processor and blend well. Using your hands, roll the mixture into 20 small balls. Put the balls on dehydrator trays, then put the trays into the dehydrator and set to 116°F/47°C for 4–6 hours. Alternatively, you can dry the balls in a normal oven with the fan on and heated to the lowest setting. Place the balls on a baking sheet, keep the oven door open with a wooden spoon, and leave for 3–4 hours.

The balls are ready when they are crunchy on the outside and soft on the inside.

Meanwhile, for the sauce, put all the ingredients into a blender, add ⅓ cup (2½ fl oz/75 ml) water, and blend well. Set aside.

Transfer the falafel balls to a serving bowl, garnish with parsley and serve the sauce in a bowl on the side. To eat, place 2 falafel balls on a wrap or lettuce leaf with some fermented carrots and the sesame seed sauce.

Taco with Avocado and Sour Cashew "Cream"

Serves 4

- 2 large turnips, peeled and cut into thin slices
- 1 tablespoon lemon juice
- 1 tablespoon olive oil

For the sour cashew "cream"
- 1 cup (5 oz/150 g) cashews
- 4 tablespoons lime juice
- 1 tablespoon nutritional yeast flakes
- ⅛ teaspoon white pepper
- ¼ teaspoon sea salt flakes

For the mashed avocado
- 2 avocados, peeled, pitted, and cut into cubes
- 2 tablespoons chopped red onion
- 2 tablespoons chopped cilantro (coriander)
- 2 tablespoons lime juice
- 1 clove garlic, chopped
- ½ teaspoon sea salt
- a pinch of freshly ground black pepper

For the nut "meat"
- scant 1 cup (3½ oz/100 g) walnuts
- ½ teaspoon cumin powder
- ½ teaspoon onion powder
- ¼ teaspoon smoked paprika powder
- 1 tablespoon tamari sauce

To finish
- cress, to sprinkle
- small bunch long chives, for tying each taco

It's best to use a mandoline, if you have one, to cut the turnips into thin slices.

For the sour cashew "cream," put the cashew nuts into a bowl, pour in enough water to cover, and soak for 2 hours. Drain and discard the soaking water. Set aside.

Put the turnip slices into a bowl. Mix the lemon juice and olive oil together and pour over the turnip slices. Turn the turnip slices until coated, then cover and let marinate for about 10 minutes

Put the avocado into a bowl and mash with a fork. Add the onion, cilantro (coriander), lime juice, and garlic, season with the sea salt and black pepper, and mix to combine. Set aside.

For the sour cashew "cream," put the soaked cashew nuts into a blender with the remaining ingredients, add ½ cup (4 fl oz/120 ml) water, and blend until smooth. If it's too thick, add about 1 tablespoon water. Don't add too much water, otherwise it will be too thin. Set aside.

Process all of the nut "meat" ingredients in a food processor by pressing the pulse button a few times until well combined but still chunky. Set aside.

To finish, take a marinated turnip slice and bend it so that it forms a "U" shape. Put a tablespoon of the nut "meat" on it as a base, then add about 2 tablespoons mashed avocados and the cashew cream on top. Sprinkle with cress and tie it with a chive. Repeat with the remaining tacos.

Zucchini Pizza Crust

Makes 1 large or 2 small pizzas

- 3 zucchini (courgette), finely grated
- ¾ cup (2½ oz/70 g) almond flour
- ¼ cup (1 oz/30 g) grated vegetarian Parmesan-style cheese or vegan cheese
- 2 tablespoons ground chia seeds
- 1 teaspoon dried oregano
- 1 teaspoon garlic powder
- ¼ teaspoon sea salt flakes
- freshly ground black pepper

For the tomato sauce
- ¾ cup (7 oz/200 g) canned diced tomatoes
- ¼ cup (1½ oz/40 g) tomato paste (purée)
- 2 cloves garlic, finely chopped
- 1–2 teaspoons dried oregano
- sea salt flakes

For the garlic oil
- 4 tablespoons olive oil
- 4 cloves garlic, crushed
- 1 tablespoon finely chopped parsley
- 1 teaspoon chili flakes
- pinch sea salt flakes

For the topping
- ½ cup (2 oz/50 g) grated vegan cheese, or another cheese of your choice
- ½ cup (4 oz/120 g) Wild Sorrel Pesto (see page 144), optional
- 1 handful arugula (rocket)

Preheat the oven to 350°F/180°C/Gas Mark 4 and line a baking sheet with parchment (baking) paper.

Put the zucchini (courgette) into a nut milk bag or in a piece of cheesecloth (muslin) and squeeze out the excess water with your hands, discarding the water. This squeezing is important, otherwise the dough will become too wet. Put the grated zucchini in a bowl with the almond flour, cheese, chia seeds, oregano, and garlic powder. Season with the salt and black pepper and mix together. Transfer the dough to the prepared baking sheet and form into 1 large or 2 small pizza crusts (bases) by flattening the dough with your hands. Bake for 25 minutes, or until golden.

Meanwhile, prepare the tomato sauce. Mix all the ingredients together in a bowl and set aside.

For the garlic oil, put everything into a jar, seal with a lid, and shake. Set aside.

Remove the crust from the oven. Cover it with the tomato sauce and top with your chosen cheese. Put it back in the oven for another 5–10 minutes. Remove from the oven and top with the pesto, if using, arugula (rocket), and garlic oil. Enjoy.

Tip: If you are not following a nut-free diet and you have some wild sorrel pesto, you can use this as a topping for the pizza, too.

Quinoa Pizza Crust

Make 1 pizza

- ¾ cup (4 oz/115 g) quinoa
- ½ teaspoon sea salt flakes
- 1 clove garlic
- ½ teaspoon freshly ground black pepper
- 2 teaspoons dried oregano
- ¼ cup (¾ oz/20 g) grated vegan cheese
- 1 tablespoon olive oil

For the topping
- scant ½ cup (3½ oz/100 g) vegan cream cheese
- ½ zucchini (courgette), very thinly sliced
- 2–3 tablespoons pine nuts
- 3–4 sprigs rosemary
- 1 tablespoon truffle oil

Put the quinoa into a bowl, pour in enough water to cover, and let soak overnight.

The next day, preheat the oven to 375°F/190°C/Gas Mark 5 and line a baking sheet with parchment (baking) paper.

Drain and rinse the quinoa, then put it into a blender together with ¼ cup (2 fl oz/60 ml) water, the salt, garlic, black pepper, and oregano and blend until smooth. Pour the batter into a bowl and mix in the cheese and olive oil.

Put a 9 inch (23 cm) tart ring on the prepared baking sheet and pour in the quinoa batter. Bake for about 20 minutes, then remove from the oven. Wearing oven mitts (gloves), flip the crust over by covering it with another baking sheet, grasping both sides of the 2 baking sheets, and flipping the sheets with the crust between them. Bake on the second sheet for another 5–10 minutes.

Remove the crust from the oven and lower the temperature to 345°F/175°C/Gas Mark 3–4. Spread the crust with the cream cheese, top with the zucchini (courgette) slices, and sprinkle with the pine nuts. Bake for another 8 minutes.

Meanwhile, in a small skillet (frying pan) briefly cook the rosemary sprigs in the truffle oil over medium heat. When the pizza is ready, sprinkle with the fried rosemary and serve.

Vegan Burgers and Root Vegetable Fries

Serves 6

- 3 tablespoons vegetable oil, for cooking
- 1 lb 2 oz (500 g) mushrooms, thinly sliced
- 4 cloves garlic, very finely chopped
- 2 cups (11 oz/300 g) cooked black beans, rinsed and drained
- 1 sweet potato, baked and cut into cubes
- ¾ cup (2½ oz/70 g) almond flour
- ⅓ cup (1¾ oz/55 g) ground chia seeds
- 1 tablespoon smoked paprika
- 1 teaspoon salt
- 1 teaspoon onion powder
- ½ teaspoon freshly ground black pepper

For the root vegetable fries
- 1 sweet potato, peeled and cut into 2 x ¼ inch (5 x ½ cm) sticks
- 1 beet (beetroot), peeled and cut into sticks
- 1 carrot, peeled and cut into sticks
- 1 celery root (celeriac), peeled and cut into sticks
- 1 tablespoon coconut oil or vegetable oil
- 1 teaspoon paprika
- 1 teaspoon sea salt flakes

To serve
- 6 slices Homemade Seed Bread (see page 160)
- ½ avocado, sliced
- 6 cherry tomatoes, sliced
- 1 quantity Smoky Coconut (see page 178)
- 1 quantity Spicy Cashew Mayo (see page 178)
- 1 handful mâche (corn salad), to sprinkle

Heat the oven to 375°F/190°C/Gas Mark 5 and line a baking sheet with parchment (baking) paper.

For the fries, massage all the vegetables with the oil, then place them on the prepared baking sheet, sprinkle with 2 tablespoons water, and bake in the hot oven for about 20 minutes. Keep warm.

Meanwhile, heat a saucepan over medium heat. When the pan is hot, add 1 tablespoon vegetable oil and warm. Add the mushrooms and garlic, and cook for 5 minutes. Put the mushrooms into a bowl with the remaining ingredients and knead together with your hands. Divide the mixture into 6 portions and flatten them into patties with the palm of your hands. Put the patties on a plate and chill in the refrigerator for about 30 minutes.

To cook the burgers, heat 2 tablespoons oil in a skillet (frying pan) over medium heat. Add the patties and cook for 3–4 minutes on each side, or until golden on both sides.

To finish, place the burgers on the slices of seed bread and top with spicy cashew mayo, avocado slices, tomato slices, and smoky coconut. Sprinkle with the mâche (corn salad) and serve with the root vegetable fries on the side.

Smoky Coconut

Makes 1 cup (3 oz/95 g)

- 1 cup (2¾ oz/75 g) flaked coconut
- 1 tablespoon tamari
- ½ teaspoon smoked paprika
- ¼ teaspoon onion powder
- ¼ teaspoon garlic powder

Preheat the oven to 325°F/160°C/Gas Mark 3 and line a baking sheet with parchment (baking) paper.

Combine all the ingredients together in a bowl and lightly toss until everything is evenly coated. Spread the mixture out on the prepared baking sheet and bake for about 15 minutes, stirring every 5 minutes so the coconut does not burn. Remove from the oven and cool for about 15 minutes, or until crisp.

Spicy Cashew Mayo

Makes 2 cups (15½ oz/440 g)

- 1 cup (5 oz/150 g) cashew nuts
- 4 tablespoons lemon juice
- 2–3 medjool dates, pitted
- 1 tablespoon harissa or other chili paste
- 1 clove garlic
- 1 teaspoon onion powder
- a pinch of Himalayan pink salt or sea salt
- freshly ground black pepper

Put the cashew nuts into a bowl, pour in enough water to cover, and soak for 2 hours. Drain and discard the soaking water.

Put the cashew nuts into a blender with all the remaining ingredients, add ½ cup (4 fl oz/120 ml) water, and blend until smooth. Transfer to a sterilized (see page 22) glass jar and store in the refrigerator until ready to use.

Kelp Noodles with Tofu

Serves 3–4

- 1 package (about 12 oz/340g) kelp noodles
- 1 small head broccoli, cut into bite-size pieces
- 1–2 tablespoons toasted sesame oil
- 1 cup (2¾ oz/75 g) thinly sliced white cabbage
- 2 carrots, cut into thin strips
- 1 zucchini (courgette), shredded into spaghetti strips with a julienne peeler or spiralizer
- ⅓ cup (½ oz/15 g) chopped cilantro (coriander), plus extra to garnish
- ¼ cup (¼ oz/10 g) basil, chopped
- 2 tablespoons chopped mint (optional)
- 2 tablespoons finely shredded fresh ginger root
- 1 tablespoon shredded lime peel
- 3 lime leaves, cut into very fine strips

For the tofu
- 2 tablespoons tamari sauce
- 1 tablespoon honey
- 1 tablespoon roasted sesame oil
- 1 teaspoon ground or crushed ginger
- 7 oz (200 g) tofu, drained and cut into 8 pieces
- ⅓ cup (1¾ oz/50 g) toasted almonds or other nuts

For the peanut sauce
- scant ¼ cup (1¾ fl oz/50 ml) tamari
- 2 tablespoons lemon or lime juice
- 2 tablespoons peanut butter
- 1 tablespoon shredded fresh ginger root
- 1 tablespoon roasted sesame oil
- 1 tablespoon agave nectar or honey
- 1–2 cloves garlic
- fresh chile, to taste

For the tofu, put all the ingredients, except the tofu and nuts into a bowl and mix together. Brush the tofu pieces with the mixture, place in a deep plate, and marinate for 10–30 minutes. The tofu will taste better the longer you marinate it.

Preheat the oven to 400°F/200°C/Gas Mark 6.

Spread the chopped nuts out in a shallow dish or plate and roll the tofu pieces until they are coated all over, then put onto a nonstick baking sheet and bake for 6–7 minutes. Turn the tofu pieces over and bake for another for 6–7 minutes, or until golden brown.

Put the kelp noodles into a bowl, pour in enough cold water to cover, and soak for 10–15 minutes.

To make the peanut sauce, put all the ingredients into a blender and blend well. Alternatively, mix everything in a mortar with a pestle. Transfer to a clean glass jar and set aside.

Put the broccoli into a strainer (sieve), pour over boiling water, and drain. Strain the kelp noodles, let them lightly dry, and transfer to a bowl.

Heat the sesame oil in a saucepan over medium heat, add the cabbage and carrots, and cook for 4–5 minutes, or until they soften, then place in the bowl with the noodles. Add all the remaining ingredients and mix together to combine. Add the tofu and serve with the peanut sauce on the side.

Tip: If you are following a vegan diet, use agave nectar instead of honey.

Turmeric Tostada

DF V

Serves 3–4

- 2 tablespoons virgin olive oil
- 2 cloves garlic
- 2⅔ cups (14 oz/400 g) cooked black beans
- 2 teaspoons Mexican spice mix
- ½–1 teaspoon sea salt flakes
- 1 lemon
- 2–3 tablespoons cilantro (coriander)
- lime wedges, to serve

For the turmeric bread
- scant 1 cup (3½ oz/100 g) spelt flour
- 1½ teaspoons turmeric
- 1 teaspoon aluminum-free baking powder
- ½ teaspoon sea salt flakes
- 4 tablespoons almond milk
- 1 tablespoon lemon juice
- 1 tablespoon olive oil
- 1-2 tablespoons coconut oil, for frying

For the salsa
- 4 plum tomatoes, cut in half, seeded, and cut into ¼ x ¼ inch (5 x 5 mm) cubes
- 1 red bell pepper, cut in half, cored, seeded, and cut into ¼ x ¼ inch (5 x 5 mm) cubes
- seeds from 1 pomegranate
- 2 tablespoons cilantro (coriander)
- 1 tablespoon finely chopped onion
- 1 tablespoon shredded lime zest
- 1 tablespoon lime juice
- 1 tablespoon finely chopped fresh chile
- ½ teaspoon Himalaya pink salt
- freshly ground black pepper

For the guacamole
- 2 avocados, peeled and pitted
- 1 tablespoon chopped onion
- 1 tablespoon finely chopped chile
- 1 tablespoon lime juice
- 1 clove garlic, crushed
- ¼ teaspoon salt
- 3 tablespoons finely chopped cilantro (coriander)

To make the turmeric bread, sift together the flour, turmeric, baking powder, and salt into a large bowl. Add the almond milk, lemon juice, and olive oil and mix to form a dough. Knead the dough and let sit for 30 minutes. Knead again and divide into 8 balls. Roll out each ball on a floured counter to a diameter of 4–5 inches (10–12 cm).

Grease a skillet (frying pan) with coconut oil and heat. Cook each turmeric bread for 1½ minutes on each side.

For the salsa, put all the ingredients into a bowl and mix together. It's ready to serve, so set aside.

For the guacamole, put the avocado into a bowl and mash with a fork. Add all the remaining ingredients and mix together. It's now ready and can be stored in an airtight container in the refrigerator for 3–4 days.

To cook the black beans, heat the oil in a saucepan over medium heat, add the garlic, and cook for 2–3 minutes. Add the black beans and Mexican spice mix, stir until mixed, and simmer for about 5 minutes. Stir and mash the beans with the ladle while they are simmering. Season with the salt and squeeze the juice from the lemon over the beans. Remove from the heat and add the cilantro (coriander). Serve on the turmeric bread with the salsa, guacamole, and some lime wedges.

Farrotto with Orange Root Vegetables

(DF) V

Serves 3–4

- 2 sweet potatoes, peeled and cut into ¾ x ¾ inch (2 x 2 cm) cubes
- 2 carrots, peeled and cut into ¾ x ¾ inch (2 x 2 cm) cubes
- 1 butternut squash, peeled, seeded, and cut into ¾ x ¾ inch (2 x 2 cm) cubes
- 2 tablespoons coconut oil
- ⅔ cup (4 oz/120 g) farro
- 2 tablespoons olive oil
- 1 leek, chopped
- 2 tablespoons chopped sage
- 2 cups (16 fl oz/475 ml) almond milk
- 1 tablespoon curry paste
- sea salt and freshly ground black pepper
- vegan cream cheese, to serve (optional)

Preheat the oven to 400°F/200°C/Gas Mark 6.

In a large roasting pan, toss the root vegetable cubes in the coconut oil and season with salt and pepper. Spread the vegetable cubes out in an even layer, and roast in the oven, stirring occasionally, for about 30 minutes, or until tender.

Meanwhile, combine the farro with 4 cups (32 fl oz/ 950 ml) water in a saucepan and bring to a boil. Reduce the heat and simmer for 25 minutes. Drain and return to the pan.

Heat the olive oil in a large skillet (frying pan) over medium heat. Add the leek and cook for 5 minutes. Stir in the sage, season with sea salt and freshly ground black pepper, and cook for 2–3 minutes. Add the farro and stir in the almond milk, then add the curry paste and simmer until all the milk has been absorbed. Remove from the heat and stir in the root vegetables. Season with salt and pepper and serve with cream cheese, if using.

Evening/Dinner/A Little More Time

Winter Recipes and Activities

Growing Greens Indoors

In Iceland, during the winter when the backyards, gardens, and balconies are asleep under a white blanket of snow, our green thumbs are itching to do a project. It is very rewarding to let home-grown greens into your life in the cold season. Sunflower and buckwheat greens are one of the easiest and quickest plants to grow indoors. They are small nutritious plants filled with chlorophyll. Sunflower sprouts are full of chlorophyll, which in a way you can call a "liquid sunlight." It benefits many functions within the body, keeping our blood healthy by reducing inflammation and calming the nervous system. We like to use them in everything—salads, smoothies, sandwiches—or as an attractive garnish to warm comforting dishes. Children like to help with these kinds of projects and will probably eat more of the greens that they have helped grow themselves.

Easy Winter Indoor Greens

- 9 oz (250 g) sunflower or buckwheat
  seeds with husks
- 1 clean 1 quart (34 fl oz/1 liter) jar
- 1 nylon mesh
- 1 rubber band
- 2 seed flats (sprouting trays)
- soil mix (compost)

Put the seeds and water into a large bowl (you need 1 part seeds to 4 parts water) and soak for 6–8 hours, or overnight, then rinse and drain.

Place the seeds in the jar, cover with the nylon mesh, and secure with a rubber band. Place the jar upside down on a drying rack for 1–2 days (or you can prop the jar at an angle with the screen facing down, so any excess water can drain off), washing and rinsing twice each day. Rinse by filling the jar to cover the seeds, swish the water around to rinse all the sprouts, then drain through the screen top. When the sprouts have grown to about ⅛ inch (2–3 mm), they are ready to plant.

Fill two-thirds of a seed flat (sprouting tray) with soil mix (compost). Water the soil mix and place the sprouts on the surface, closely together. Cover by placing the other seed flat on top as a lid (or you can use a dark plastic bag and cut holes in it for air instead, if you want). The dark helps the sprouts to make roots.

After 3 days, remove the lid or plastic bag and place the seed flat in a bright place—either on a sunny windowsill or use indoor grow lights. Water daily until the greens have reached 4–5 inches (12–15 cm), then they are ready to use.

Holiday Presents Homemade and Upcycled

One of the most valuable gifts we can give our family and friends is our time, so a good idea is to make a homemade gift card to arrange a date or a day that you can share with your family and friends. It can be anything. Let your imagination loose—arrange a beautiful picnic, go swimming, cook a special meal, or go to the theater—the possibilities are endless. Enjoy being together because most of the time great experiences give more happiness in the long run than expensive store-bought items. Here are some present ideas to make for the holidays.

Cleaning Jars with Homemade Scrub

- 2 tablespoons baking soda (bicarbonate of soda)
  or 2 tablespoons sea salt flakes
- scant ¼ cup (1¾ fl oz/50 ml) olive oil

We're obsessed with finding new purposes for old things and we rescue all our old jars and use them for everything. Some types of glue are stubborn and make cleaning and reusing jars a hard job. We have discovered how to get rid of even the most difficult labels and glue stains. Here is our method:

Combine the baking soda (bicarbonate of soda) or salt and olive oil and keep in a clean jar with a lid for future use.

Soak the jars you want to clean in warm soapy water for 4–5 hours, or overnight (don't throw away the water, because you can reuse it).

Use the hard part of your dishwashing brush to peel off as much of the label as possible. If there is still some glue and label on the jar, now is the time to take out the oil scrub.

Rub the scrub on the glue stains on the jar. Let stand for about an hour if the stains are very difficult. Rub off the scrub with your dishwashing brush or with the coarse side of a dishwashing sponge, rinse the oil off with the soapy water, and ta da! Your jars are now clean and ready to use.

Upcycled Takeout Coffee Cup

- crochet needle
- cotton yarn
- clean jar with lid (see left)

Grandma Hildur likes to make sure everyone in the family is kept warm. She knits hand warmers for her great-grandchildren and even knitted a warmer for her kettle. She also likes to crochet warmers for the jars we use as takeout coffee cups. A relatively small amount of yarn is needed for each jar, so this is a good project for using up leftover yarn. Here is Grandma Hildur's method:

Find a crochet needle that fits your yarn, but don't worry too much—this project does not require high precision. Because jars come in all sizes and we like to be able to make a cozy warmer for all of them, it is good to be a little flexible with the method and follow your instincts.

Begin by cleaning a jar that you feel is the perfect size for a takeout coffee or tea. We start with the bottom of the warmer by making a crochet circle—the number of rounds will depend on the size of the bottom of your jar. When you have a circle that fits the jar bottom, you are ready to start merging it into a cylinder shape.

For the circle: Start by making a chain of 4 stitches. Now form a small ring by hooking to the first stitch with a slip stitch. Then make 2 chains.

First round in the circle: make 11 half double (UK half treble) crochets (HDC) in the ring, then 2 chains.

Second round: Make 2 double (UK treble) crochets (DC) in every HDC (total of 22 DC). Then make 2 chains. Repeat the second round until your circle fits the bottom of the jar. Then you are ready to merge your bottom circle into a cylinder form.

Join with a slip stitch and make 1 single (UK double) chain (SC) in every DC. Repeat until the cup is the desired height. Secure and it's ready to use.

Chocolate Cookies

Makes 8–10 cookies

- 2 cups (8 oz/225 g) gluten-free rolled oats
- 1 cup (8 oz/225 g) coconut palm sugar
- 2 tablespoons ground chia seeds
- 3–4 tablespoons water
- 3 tablespoons coconut oil, melted
- 1 teaspoon vanilla powder
- ¼ teaspoon sea salt flakes
- ¼ teaspoon red pepper (chili) flakes
- 1 cup (6 oz/175 g) coarsely chopped semisweet (plain) chocolate

Hildur and I like to make edible holiday gifts, and making chocolate cookies is one of our favorite ideas. The trick is to make them look nice and festive by tying them with a pretty string or bow.

Preheat the oven to 345°F/175°C/Gas Mark 3–4. Line a baking sheet with parchment (baking) paper.

Put the oats into a food processor and process until finely ground. Transfer to a bowl, add the remaining ingredients, except the chocolate, and mix together. Add the chocolate and combine.

Using a tablespoon, place spoonfuls of the cookie dough on the prepared baking sheet, making sure that they are 1½ inches (4 cm) apart, because they will spread during baking. Bake for 10–12 minutes, or until golden. Remove from the oven and cool on a wire rack—well, they might get finished before they are completely cold ...

Adzuki Bean Mask

- ½ cup (3½ oz/100 g) dried adzuki beans

This is an old Geisha beauty tip for a clean and healthy glow.

Put the beans into a clean coffee or spice grinder and grind until they become a fine powder. Store in a sterilized (see page 22) glass jar with a tight-fitting lid.

To make a single portion of mask, mix together 1 tablespoon of the adzuki bean powder and 1 teaspoon water and use immediately. Apply the mask to your clean face and leave on for 5–10 minutes, or until it feels like your skin starts to tighten. Rinse the mask off with lukewarm water.

Anytime

Desserts

A Small Sweet Treat

Everyone knows that we can't live on candies (sweets) alone, but that doesn't mean we have to feel guilty for enjoying small treats from time to time. They make life more colorful and lift our spirits.

Some desserts should be reserved for festive occasions while others can be enjoyed any time you want. We like to use healthy ingredients, like nuts, fruits, and whole grains, when we make candies, and healthy fats, such as olive oil and avocado. We often try to keep our desserts moderately sweet, and it is something that we can train our taste buds to eventually enjoy. In our opinion, it is better to gradually use less natural sugars instead of switching to artificial sweeteners that have no caloric value. This is because sweeteners keep our sweet tooth wanting more candies and other sweet foods. We think it is a healthier approach to look at candies and sweet food as something to be enjoyed in moderation. If moderation is hard, try to adapt your taste buds gradually to a less sweet taste.

When making desserts, we find that raw inspired recipes are best to make, because they require no particular skills other than knowing how to blend and press dough into molds. There's no precise chemistry, leavening, exact temperatures, or timings.

Many classic dessert recipes contain more sugar than really is necessary, and usually you can just use a little less without anyone noticing. There are also a few tricks that can come in handy when trying to reduce sugar intake. Recipes with chocolate chips or raisins don't require the dough to be as sweet, and when we use spices like cinnamon, cardamom, and vanilla, we can also use less sweeteners. Those spices add sweet flavor to the recipes, so your taste buds need less sugar to be satisfied. Trading sugar for dried fruit, date paste, applesauce (apple puree), or mashed bananas is also a good option and we encourage everyone to experiment and have fun. Be careful though: It is easiest to swap liquid for liquid and dry matter for dry matter, because of the chemistry in baking, so if you would like to make some small changes, remember to take into account the physical properties of the ingredients.

In this chapter, there are some basic recipes for butters and pastes, which can be used when making the desserts that follow; there are recipes that are ideal for everyday, such as Ginger Pears (see page 216), and ones that are decadent, like Raspberry Tart (see page 222)—a great centerpiece.

Just remember that when you decide to treat yourself with sweet dishes, it's absolutely necessary to enjoy every single bite.

Chocolate

Makes 1¾ cups (15 fl oz/450 ml)

- ½ cup (3¾ oz/110 g) almond butter
- ½ cup (3¾ oz/110 g) cacao butter or coconut oil
- ½ cup (2¼ oz/60 g) raw cacao powder
- ¼ cup (3 oz/80 g) maple syrup

We pour this mix into molds to make our own raw chocolate but you can also use it in a liquid state and use it more like a sauce or frosting. Use tahini instead of almond butter for a nut-free option.

Choose either cacao butter or coconut oil depending on what you are using the chocolate for. If using cacao butter, it will become similar to real chocolate; if using coconut oil, it becomes softer and is great for frosting. Melt the cacao butter in a double boiler or in a heatproof bowl set over a saucepan of gently simmering water. Make sure the bottom of the bowl doesn't touch the water. Add the cacao powder and maple syrup and stir together.

Coconut Butter

Makes 1⅓ cups (11 oz/300 g)

- 2⅔ cups (7 oz/200 g) shredded coconut
- 1–2 tablespoons coconut oil

This butter is beautiful in smoothies, frostings, and fillings. It makes them thick or creamy. We use it instead of heavy (double) cream or nut butter.

Put the coconut into a food processor and process for 3 minutes, stopping now and then to scrape the sides down with a rubber spatula. Each time you stop, add ½–1 tablespoon coconut oil. Repeat until it is a creamy and smooth butter. Transfer to sterilized (see page 22) jars and store in the refrigerator for up to 2 weeks. It will become firm in the refrigerator, so remove 1–2 hours before using.

Date Paste

Makes 2 cups (15 oz/450 g)

- 1 lb 2 oz (500 g) medjool dates
- a pinch of salt

If the dates are not super-soft, soak them in a bowl of water for 10–15 minutes. Pit the dates, place them in a food processor, and blend until smooth. Store the paste in an airtight container in the refrigerator. The paste can be kept for several weeks and stored in the freezer for up to 2 months. We use it as a sweetener.

Anytime / Desserts / A Small Sweet Treat

Egg Replacer

Makes the equivalent of 1 extra-large (UK large) egg for baking

- 1 tablespoon ground chia seeds

More and more people are avoiding eggs in their diet. There are many reasons for this and the most common are allergies and people avoiding animal products. Eggs play a big role in many recipes: they bind the recipe together or make the dough fluffier. Homemade egg replacer is really easy to make and here is our favorite recipe. This egg replacer gives the best result where you need a binder in the recipe.

Put the chia seeds into a coffee grinder and grind until ground. You can also use a high-speed blender. Transfer the ground chia seeds to a bowl, add 3 tablespoons water, and stir until smooth. It will keep for up to 2 weeks in the refrigerator in an airtight container.

Caramel

Makes 1½ cups (12 fl oz/350 ml)

- ⅔ cup (7 oz/200 g) coconut nectar, coconut palm sugar, or maple syrup
- ½ cup (3½ oz/100 g) coconut oil
- ¼ cup (2½ oz/65 g) almond butter
- 1 teaspoon sea salt flakes

If you woud like the caramel to be darker in color, add 1–2 teaspoons raw cacao powder. In this recipe, we like to use ⅔ cup (5 fl oz/150 ml) coconut nectar, coconut palm sugar, or maple syrup, which enhances the caramel taste. It can be used in frostings, as a topping for raw cakes, in drinks, and in all recipes that call for for caramel. This is a healthier version of the typical sugar/butter caramel.

Put all the ingredients into a blender and blend until smooth. It will keep for up to 2 weeks in the refrigerator in an airtight container.

Nut Bites

Makes 20 nut bites

For the caramel layer
- ⅔ cup (3¼ oz/90 g) coconut nectar or sweetener of your choice
- ⅓ cup (2½ oz/75 g) coconut oil
- ⅓ cup (2¾ oz/75 g) almond butter
- 1 teaspoon sea salt flakes
- ½ teaspoon ground turmeric

For the chocolate topping
- ½ cup (3½ oz/100 g) coconut oil
- ½ cup (3¾ oz/110 g) almond butter
- ½ cup (2 oz/60 g) raw cacao powder
- ¼ cup (3 oz/80 g) coconut nectar or maple syrup

For the nut layer
- 5 oz (150 g) medjool dates, pitted
- generous ¾ cup (4 oz/125 g) pecans
- ¼ teaspoon sea salt flakes

For the second layer
- 1⅓ cups (11 oz/300 g) peanut butter

To make the caramel layer, put all the ingredients into a blender and blend until smooth. Set aside.

For the chocolate topping, melt the coconut oil and almond butter in a double boiler or in a heatproof bowl set over a saucepan of gently simmering water. Make sure the bottom of the bowl doesn't touch the water. Stir in the cacao powder and coconut nectar until smooth and set aside.

For the nut layer, put all the ingredients into a food processor and blend until sticky. Press the mixture into a 12 x 12 inch (30 x 30 cm) baking pan and freeze for 15 minutes. It will be easier to spread the peanut butter over the nut layer when the crust is cold and firm.

Spread the peanut butter evenly over the nut layer. Spread the caramel layer over the top of the peanut butter, then top with the chocolate. Freeze until firm, then cut into 1¼ x 1¼ inch (3 x 3 cm) squares.

Anytime/Desserts/A Small Sweet Treat

Avocado Truffles

Makes 12 truffles

- 7 oz (200 g) semisweet (plain) chocolate, at least 70% cocoa solids
- 2 avocados, peeled and pitted
- coconut oil, for oiling
- raw cacao powder, for rolling

These truffles are so easy and simple to make. We made this recipe originally as a simple healthy frosting for a cake, but the batch was too big so we used the leftover frosting to make truffles. You will be pleasantly surprised if you try them. Pick your favorite chocolate, either semisweet (plain) or bittersweet (dark) with orange, peppermint, or a flavor of your choice. The truffles can be covered with chopped nuts, shredded coconut, or orange zest. For a raw option, you can use raw chocolate or raw homemade chocolate (see page 202).

Melt the chocolate in a double boiler or in a heatproof bowl set over a saucepan of gently simmering water. Make sure the bottom of the bowl doesn't touch the water. Remove from the heat and pour into a food processor. Add the avocados and, using the pulse button, blend together to a paste. Transfer the paste to a bowl, cover, and chill in the refrigerator for 30 minutes until stiff.

Using lightly oiled hands, roll the mixture into small balls. Spread the cacao powder out on a plate, then roll the balls in the cacao powder until coated. Store in an airtight container in the refrigerator or the freezer for up to 2 months.

Orange Truffles

Makes 12 truffles

- 2 cups (11 oz/300 g) medjool dates, pitted
- 2 oz (50 g) orange-flavored raw chocolate, chopped
- 3 tablespoons raw cacao powder
- 2 tablespoons coconut oil
- 1 tablespoon orange zest
- ½ teaspoon sea salt flakes
- ¼ teaspoon cayenne pepper
- oil, for oiling

For coating
- 1 tablespoon raw cacao powder
- scant 1¼ cups (4 oz/120 g) chopped pistachios

Put the dates into a food processor with all the remaining ingredients, except the oil, and using the pulse button, blend until it forms a sticky smooth paste.

Using lightly oiled hands, roll the paste into small balls. Spread the cacao powder and pistachios out on separate plates and roll the balls in one or the other, until coated. Store in an airtight container in the refrigerator for up to 3 weeks or in the freezer for up to 2 months.

Anytime/Desserts/A Small Sweet Treat

Black Bean Brownies

Makes 20 brownies

- ⅓ cup (2 oz/60 g) ground chia seeds
- 1¾ cups (12 oz/350 g) coconut palm sugar
- ⅓ cup (2¾ oz/75 g) coconut oil, plus extra to grease
- ½ cup (2 oz/60 g) cocoa powder
- ½ cup (1¾ oz/50 g) almond flour
- 1 teaspoon aluminum-free baking powder
- 1 teaspoon vanilla powder
- ¼ teaspoon sea salt flakes
- 7 oz (200 g) white chocolate, chopped
- ¾ cup (2¾ oz/75 g) pistachios, dry-roasted and chopped
- Caramel, to serve (see page 204)

For the bean paste
- 2 x 14 oz/400 g cans cooked black beans; or 1 cup (6¾ oz/190 g) dried black beans
- 1 kombu strip or ½ teaspoon baking soda (bicarbonate of soda), optional

Many years ago, when we tasted a bean cake for the first time, we discovered that it was a great dessert and were pleasantly surprised when we learned that the main ingredient was bean. Beans are a traditional ingredient in many sweet dishes in Asia. Adzuki beans are most commonly used, but here we have used black beans. If you would like a very smooth texture, then make the beans into a paste, otherwise just use the whole beans.

For the bean paste, you can either use canned or home-cooked beans. For home-cooked beans, rinse them, put into a bowl, pour in 4 cups (32 fl oz/950 ml) water, add the kombu strip or baking soda (bicarbonate of soda), and soak overnight.

The next day, drain the beans and discard the soaking water. Put the beans into a large saucepan with enough water to cover them plus ¾ inch (2 cm) extra. Bring to a boil, then reduce the heat and simmer for 1½ hours until the beans are very tender and you can mash a bean with your fingers. Turn off the heat and let cool for 10 minutes.

Now press the beans through a strainer (sieve) to separate the skins from the paste. This recipe will yield about 1½ cups (9 oz/250 g) of bean paste.

Preheat the oven to 345°F/175°C/Gas Mark 4 and grease an 8 x 8 inch (20 x 20 cm) square cake pan.

Put the ground chia seeds into a bowl, add ⅔ cup (5 fl oz/150 ml) water and stir to make a paste.

Process the bean paste in a food processor until smooth. Add the remaining ingredients, except the chocolate and pistachios, and process to a smooth batter. Add the chocolate and pistachios and blend briefly. Pour into the prepared cake pan and bake for 50–60 minutes.

Serve with caramel. If not serving immediately, store in the refrigerator.

Tip: Soaking the beans with kombu, or baking soda (bicarbonate of soda) helps make them easier to digest. When you have finished soaking the kombu, dry it and keep for future use.

Anytime/Desserts/A Small Sweet Treat

Strawberry Ice Cream

Serves 4–6

- 3 frozen bananas
- 3½ cups (1 lb 2 oz/500 g) frozen strawberries
- 2 tablespoons lemon juice
- natural sweetener, to taste (optional)

A frozen banana is a smart thing to have in your freezer because then you can make ice cream in just few minutes. Frozen bananas make the ice cream creamy and they are very sweet so you do not really need any other sweetener. The easiest recipe is just using frozen bananas; but adding some cacao powder or vanilla also makes a great but simple ice cream. You can use any frozen fruits you like and by simply adding a banana, you will make your ice cream rich and creamy.

Put all the ingredients into a food processor and blend until smooth. It's ready to serve.

Anytime/Desserts/A Small Sweet Treat

Vanilla Ice Cream

Serves 4–6

- 1⅔ cups (9 oz/250 g) cashew nuts
- 1½ cups (12 fl oz/350 ml) almond milk
- ½ cup (3½ oz/100 g) coconut palm sugar
- 1 teaspoon vanilla powder
- ¼ teaspoon sea salt flakes

For this recipe, you can use a sweetener of your choice. If you would like to add something extra, then why not add chopped chocolate, caramel, or fruit? You could even add 1 teaspoon maca or lucuma powder, or bee pollen if you want to.

Put the cashew nuts into a bowl, pour in enough water to cover, and leave to soak for 2–4 hours, or overnight. Drain and discard the soaking water.

Put the cashew nuts into a blender or food processor with all the remaining ingredients and blend or process until smooth. (If using a blender, the mixture will be very smooth and grain free—if using a food processor, the mixture will be a little grainy.) Pour the mixture into an ice-cream maker and process according to the manufacturer's instructions. Alternatively, if you don't have such a smart machine, spoon the mixture into a 9 x 5-inch/23 x 12½-cm loaf pan or silicon mold and freeze. You may have to remove from the freezer and stir 1–2 times to prevent the ice cream from eparating. Transfer the ice cream to a freezerproof container and keep frozen until ready to serve.

Anytime/Desserts/A Small Sweet Treat

Ginger Pears

Serves 4

- 1 cup (9 fl oz/250 ml) apple juice
- 2 inch (5 cm) piece fresh ginger root, peeled
- 5–10 green cardamom pods
- 2–3 star anise
- 1–2 cinnamon sticks
- 1 vanilla bean (pod), optional
- 1 unwaxed mandarin, peeled and sliced horizontally
- 4 pears, peeled, cut in half lengthwise, and cored
- Vanilla Ice Cream (see page 214), to serve, (optional)

These ginger pears are delicious with homemade vanilla ice cream.

Pour the apple juice into a saucepan and add the ginger, green cardamom, star anise, cinnamon stick, and vanilla bean (pod), if using. Bring to a boil, then, using a spoon, put the mandarin slices on the bottom of the pan and arrange the pear halves on the top. Reduce the heat and simmer for 20 minutes.

Anytime/Desserts/A Small Sweet Treat

Green Cake to Live For

Serves 10

For the crust
- 1 cup (3½ oz/100 g) walnuts
- ½ cup (2¼ oz/60 g) raw cacao powder
- ¼ teaspoon sea salt flakes
- 1½ cups (7 oz/200 g) medjool dates, pitted
- ¾ cup (4 oz/120 g) raw pistachios, coarsely chopped

For the filling
- 1 cup (5 oz/150 g) cashew nuts
- 2 avocados, peeled, halved, pitted, and cut into cubes
- 1 handful of spinach
- ¼ teaspoon chlorella
- 1 cup (9 fl oz/250 ml) almond milk
- ½ cup (5½ oz/160 g) maple syrup or coconut nectar
- ⅓ cup (2½ fl oz/75 ml) lime juice
- 1 tablespoon lime zest
- pinch of cayenne pepper
- ½ teaspoon ground cardamom powder
- ⅛ teaspoon sea salt

To serve
- chlorella, to taste

Line a 9 inch (23 cm) round springform cake pan or mold with parchment (baking) paper.

For the filling, put the cashew nuts into a bowl, pour in enough water to cover, and then soak for 2–4 hours, or overnight, then drain and discard the soaking water.

Put the avocados and cashews in a blender with the remaining filling ingredients and blend for about 30 seconds, or until smooth.

For the crust (base), put the walnuts, cacao powder, and sea salt flakes into a food processor and process until the nuts are finely ground. Add the dates, one at a time, through the feed tube of the food processor while it is running on slow speed or pulse after each addition. The mixture is ready when it sticks together. Put the mixture into a bowl and combine with the chopped pistachios. Press the mixture into the prepared cake pan or mold, pour the filling over the crust until it is completely covered, and chill in the refrigerator or freeze until ready to serve. Just before serving, sprinkle with chlorella.

Anytime/Desserts/A Small Sweet Treat

Layered Cake with Chocolate Frosting

Serves 10–12

For the cake layer
- 3 cups (1 lb/450 g) pecans
- 2 tablespoons hemp seeds
- ⅔ cup (3 oz/80 g) raw cacao powder
- 2 teaspoons vanilla powder
- 1 teaspoon cayenne pepper
- a pinch of sea salt
- 20 medjool dates, pitted and chopped
- 3 tablespoons coconut oil

For the raspberry jam
- 4 cups (1 lb 2 oz/500 g) frozen raspberries
- ¾ cup (3½ oz/100 g) mulberries
- 3 tablespoons chia seeds
- 1 teaspoon vanilla powder
- 1 teaspoon cayenne pepper
- a pinch of salt

For the banana layer
- 4 bananas, peeled and thinly sliced

For the frosting
- 14 oz (400 g) raw semisweet (plain) chocolate, broken into pieces
- 4 avocados, peeled, pitted, and mashed with a fork

To decorate
- apple flowers (when in season), otherwise use fresh berries

For the best results, make the frosting just before you are spreading it on the cake.

For the cake layer, put the pecans, hemp seeds, and cacao powder into a food processor and, using the pulse button, pulse until the nuts are coarsely ground. Add the vanilla powder, cayenne pepper, and sea salt and pulse to blend. Add the dates, a few at a time, down the feed tube while the food processor is running. Add the coconut oil and pulse a few times to blend. The mixture should stick together without getting too sticky.

Divide the cake mixture into 3 equal portions and press lightly into 3 7-inch (18-cm) round cake pans with your fingertips, making sure it covers the bottom of each pan in an even layer. Store in the refrigerator while making the raspberry jam.

For the jam, put all the ingredients into a food processor and, using the pulse button, pulse until it is coarsely ground and mixed.

To assemble the cake, remove all the chilled cake layers from the pans. Place one cake layer on a plate, spread with a layer of banana slices, then a layer of raspberry jam, then another cake layer, then another layer of banana slices, raspberry jam, and repeat with the remaining ingredients.

Place the layered cake in the freezer for 15 minutes before covering it with the frosting because the best way to spread the frosting is when the cake is cold.

For the frosting, melt the chocolate in a double boiler or in a heatproof bowl set over a pan of gently simmering water. Make sure the bottom of the bowl doesn't touch the water. Put the chocolate and the avocado into a food processor and mix until smooth.

Remove the cake from the freezer and cover with the frosting. Decorate with apple flowers or plenty of your favorite fresh berries.

Anytime/Desserts/A Small Sweet Treat

Raspberry Tart

Serves 10–12

- 1 cup (5 oz/150 g) almonds
- scant 1 cup (3½ oz/100 g) walnuts
- 2 cups (12 oz/350 g) medjool dates, pitted
- ½ teaspoon vanilla powder
- 2 tablespoons orange zest, grated

For the filling
- 11 oz/300 g raw white chocolate
- ½ cup (2 oz/50 g) cacao butter
- 2 cups (7 oz/200 g) raspberries
- ¼ cup (1½ oz/40 g) ground chia seeds
- 2 tablespoons beet (beetroot) juice

For the raspberry layer
- 2 cups (9 oz/250 g) fresh or frozen raspberries

For the crumb topping
- ¾ cup (3½ oz/100 g) dried mulberries
- 2 tablespoons coconut palm sugar

This delicious tart is always a winner. You can either make one big one or loads of muffin-size individual tarts. The large tart is best served immediately, because it tends to melt if kept too long on the table, but the little ones are much more resilient.

For the filling, melt the chocolate and the cacao butter in a double boiler or in a heatproof bowl set over a saucepan of gently simmering water. Set aside.

Line a 9 inch (23 cm) round baking pan with parchment (baking) paper.

Chop the almonds and walnuts and put into a food processor and coarsely grind. Add the dates and vanilla to the food processor and blend to a sticky dough. Add the orange zest and, using the pulse button, pulse 2–3 times. Press into the prepared pan with your fingertips, making sure it covers the bottom of the pan in an even layer, and freeze while making the filling.

To make the filling, put all the ingredients into a food processor and process until smooth.

To assemble the tart, spread the raspberries on the crust and pour the filling over to cover the raspberries. Store in the freezer for 3–4 hours or in the refrigerator overnight, until the filling is firm.

Meanwhile, put the crumb topping ingredients into a food processor and process until almost a fine flour crumb. When the tart filling has set, sprinkle with the crumb topping.

Tip: If you are not following a raw-food diet, add an extra nutty flavor to your tart by dry-roasting the almonds and walnuts in a saucepan over medium heat for 3–4 minutes, or until golden brown. Keep an eye on them, because they can burn easily. Remove from the heat and cool slightly before chopping them. Let cool completely.

Anytime/Desserts/A Small Sweet Treat

Cheesecake with Blueberries

Serves 10–12

For the filling
- 3 cups (1 lb/450 g) cashew nuts
- ¾ cup (8½ oz/240 g) maple syrup
- 4 tablespoons lemon juice
- 2 teaspoons vanilla powder
- 2 teaspoons probiotic powder
- ⅛ teaspoon sea salt
- ¾ cup (5½ oz/160 g) coconut oil
- 2 tablespoons ground chia seed

For the crust
- 1 cup (5 oz/150 g) pecans
- 2 cups (10 oz/280 g) dried mulberries
- ¼ cup (2¼ fl oz/60 ml) coconut oil, liquefied
- a pinch of sea salt

For the topping
- 1 cup (10 oz/275 g) Wild Berry Jam (see page 154)
- 1 cup (5 oz/150 g) fresh blueberries

Line a 9 inch (23 cm) round cake pan with parchment (baking) paper.

For the filling, put the cashew nuts into a bowl, pour in enough water to cover, and soak for about 2 hours. Drain and discard the soaking water. Set aside.

To make the crust (base), put the pecans, mulberries, oil, and salt into a food processor and blend until it all sticks together but is still a little coarse. Press the mixture into the prepared pan with your fingertips. Make sure it covers the bottom of the pan in an even layer.

To make the filling, put the drained cashew nuts into a high-speed blender or food processor with the maple syrup, lemon juice, vanilla, probiotic powder, and salt and blend. Add the coconut oil and chia seed and blend briefly. Pour the mixture over the crust and chill overnight in the refrigerator or for 3-4 hours in the freezer until the filling is firm. Top with a layer of blueberry jam and fresh blueberries and serve.

Anytime/Desserts/A Small Sweet Treat

Ingredients and Equipment

ACAI BERRY POWDER
Acai berries come from the acai palm, which is native to Central and South America where they are prized for their nutritional value. Dried and then ground, this dark purple powder has a deep fruity, some say chocolaty flavor, and are packed with antioxidants and vitamins to support the immune system, plus essential omega fatty acids.

ADZUKI BEANS
As with most beans, these are a protein and fiber-packed treat, but it's the distinct sweetness and color of the adzuki bean that makes it such a valuable ingredient, particularly in Japanese cuisine. The beans are about half the size of kidney beans and used whole as well as in a paste. As with most dried beans, they need thorough cooking before use.

AGAVE NECTAR
Drawn from the fleshy agave cactus, this sweet syrup is a useful vegan substitute for honey. It is sweeter than sugar, meaning you can use less of it, however, it is very high in fructose, so is best enjoyed in moderation.

ALMOND BUTTER
Ground whole, roasted almonds make a heavenly alternative to peanut butter. We use almond butter to bind pie dough and baking batters and to add body to dressings and drinks. Nut butters from "activated" nuts (see Soaking Nuts, page 235)—i.e. those that have been soaked, sprouted, and dried before they are ground—are the most nutritious.

ALMOND FLOUR
Almond flour is made from very finely ground almonds that have had some of their oil removed. You can make your own if you have made almond milk and can dehydrate the remaining pulp. This is not to be confused with ground almonds, which is coarser and has a more oily, damp feel.

ALUMINUM-FREE BAKING POWDER
Most baking powders are "double acting." This means they contain an acid that reacts with the alkali component of the powder (baking soda/bicarbonate of soda) to create bubbles, plus an acid that reacts with the heat of the oven to create even more of a rise. Some brands use sodium aluminum sulfate (sulphate) or phosphate as this second acid. Baked goods made with either of these can have a distinctly metallic taste, so pick an aluminum-free brand.

ASHWAGANDHA
Native to India, the aswagandha plant is from the same family as the tomato and used as an herb in Ayurvedic medicine. The root is dried, then ground to a powder. Known as Indian ginseng, it is thought not only to improve energy levels and immunity but also calm and help tackle anxiety, stress, and sleep problems.

BEE POLLEN
See a bee flying back to the hive and you will probably spot yellow balls attached to its back legs. These little packages are pollen, which can be collected and dried by the beekeeper. There are ethical arguments against the collection of bee pollen, because this highly nutritious protein source is intended (by the bees at least) for the growing hive. Do not eat bee pollen if you are pregnant, breastfeeding, following a vegan diet, or if you have experienced pollen allergies.

BEET JUICE

This ruby red juice can be bought in health food stores, but for the most healthly option, juicing it fresh is best. Beets (beetroot) are full of iron and folate (which is naturally occurring folic acid), plus studies have shown the nitrate content in beets can help to reduce blood pressure as part of a healthy diet. Use it in drinks like Pink Lemonade (see page 119) and as a natural food coloring.

BUCKWHEAT, INCLUDING SEEDS FOR SPROUTING

Don't be fooled by the name, buckwheat isn't a wheat at all. The seeds are entirely gluten free and come from a plant in the rhubarb family, historically grown in areas too hostile to sustain other cereals. Whole buckwheat seeds can easily be sprouted for use in salads, smoothies, and garnishes, providing a valuable source of greens during the winter months. Dried buckwheat makes a grayish flour easily substituted for wheat flours and is particularly delicious when combined with ground almonds.

CACAO BUTTER

Also sold as cocoa butter, this is the fatty remainder of the cocoa bean once the cocoa part has been removed. It can be used instead of butter and other fats, with particularly tasty results in chocolate making and raw baking. It will melt easily and firm up when it cools, and will give your recipe a rich chocolaty flavor and smell.

CARDAMOM POWDER

Cardamom has a very distinctive sweet, scented flavor, popular in cooking from the Indian subcontinent and also Scandinavian baking. It is said to stimulate and calm the digestive system. This spice is most commonly sold as whole, small green pods that must be split open to reveal the brownish seeds within. Cardamom loses flavor quickly once the seeds are ground. Buying already ground powder? Choose only small packages and keep well sealed in a cool, dark place.

CHIA SEEDS

Loved by the Aztecs and now used widely in raw and health food recipes, these blackish gray, poppy seed-size grains swell greatly when soaked in liquid, acting as a helpful thickening and hunger-quelling ingredient. Grinding or crushing the seeds before use helps the body to digest chia.

CHIPOTLE CHILES

These smoky dried chiles are popular in Mexican cuisine, often blended into chipotle paste. The very ripe, deep red, and already drying out chiles are picked from the bush, then dried to their familiar blackish brown and very wrinkly appearance. Soaked dried chipotles (and also canned chipotles) can be used in marinades, rubs, and salsas, and have a rounded flavor that is medium instead of overpoweringly hot.

CHLORELLA

This microalgae is extremely high in protein, essential fatty acids, vitamins, and minerals and is ideal for enhancing your morning smoothie. Chlorella comes packaged as a green powder, or in pill form, the latter of which can easily be crushed. As the name suggests, chlorella is full of chlorophyll—this is the algae that turns lakes green after all—and is a powerful antioxidant.

COCONUT BUTTER

This is a rich, buttery, and very nutty product that contains a lot of shredded coconut meat to give a creamy texture. Do not confuse it with coconut oil, which looks similar at room temperature in the package but is actually pure fat from the coconut. Use coconut butter as a spread, to thicken and enrich smoothies, and to make frostings (icings) and candies (sweets).

COCONUT NECTAR

This sweet sap is extracted from the flowering part of the coconut palm and needs no lengthy heat treatment to concentrate its flavor (unlike maple and agave syrups). It therefore retains more enzymes and nutrients within and is considered a "raw" food. Nectar doesn't have any coconut flavor but an all round sweetness I find really useful in the kitchen. It has a low glycemic index (GI) and a low fructose content, which can make it a healthier choice when choosing a sweetener.

COCONUT PALM SUGAR

This is simply coconut nectar that has been dried into crystals. Again, this granulated palm sugar doesn't have a coconut flavor, but a light caramel, floral sweetness similar to light brown sugar. Use in baking.

COCONUT WATER

Shake a fresh coconut and you will hear coconut water sloshing around within it. Different to coconut milk and creams, which are a product of soaking the coconut flesh (and often high in fat), coconut water is low fat and refreshing, with a good balance of electrolytes and carbohydrates but less sugar than most energy or sports drinks. It has a lightly sweet, nutty flavor and can be used instead in drinks, soups, ices, and more.

COLD-PRESSED OLIVE OIL

To make high-quality oil, olives are crushed at low temperatures, which helps to retain its health-giving properties. Olive oil contains high levels of monounsaturated fats, which have a protective effect on health. Store cold-pressed oils in a dark, cool place, because they deteriorate quickly when exposed to light and heat.

CHAGA MUSHROOM EXTRACT POWDER

This tastes and smells similar to coffee and can easily be used as a coffee substitute that is high in antioxidants but without the caffeine. Its origin, however, couldn't be more different to coffee. Chaga fungus can be found growing in the Northern hemisphere, specifically on beech trees. The fungus is dried then milled to a fine powder, which is then ready to use.

CREAM WHIPPER

Looking like a soda syphon, a cream whipper is a sealed flask loaded with nitrous oxide from special cartridges. The cream (or any liquid thick enough to hold bubbles) is held under high pressure in the flask. As it is propelled out of the whipper, the pressure in the liquid drops dramatically, causing the dissolved gas within it to emerge as bubbles—and your cream to come out as foam. It is available from specialty kitchen suppliers.

CROWBERRIES

These small dark, bluish black berries are indigenous to Iceland, Alaska, and Canada. Like most small berries, they are contain plenty of vitamin C and antioxidants and are a welcome source in colder climates where other berries and fruits can't flourish. Crowberries are ideal for jam making and baking, because cooking enhances their flavor. Substitute with blackberries or blueberries, if needed.

DEHYDRATOR

This machine slowly removes the water from food, drying it out and concentrating flavors as it goes. It is very useful if you would like to preserve a glut of fruit, or for drying activated nuts (see Soaked nuts, page 235), making kale chips, homemade crackers, and granola. If you don't have a dehydrator, you can set your oven to its lowest temperature, keep the fan on, and then place a wooden spoon in the oven door for ventilation.

DULSE

This red seaweed can be enjoyed fresh or dried, as a vegetable ingredient or a snack by itself. Seaweeds are highly nutritious and slightly salty, containing a lot of trace elements and protein. Dulse is a natural flavor enhancer, too, with a natural "umami" quality, and will bring out other flavors in soups and salad dressings.

FARRO

Farro is an ancient strain of wheat grain, used most commonly in Italian cooking as a hearty alternative to rice and pasta in salads, soups, and stews. Similar to spelt and barley in shape and size, it has a mildly nutty flavor and retains a chewy texture when cooked. As a whole grain, it is rich in vitamins and fiber and will keep you satisfied for longer.

FLAXSEEDS AND FLAXSEED OIL

Small, flat, shiny brown seeds that are perfect in bars, breads, and granolas, flaxseeds contain one of the highest concentrations of omega-3 fatty acids in the plant world—ideal if you don't eat oily fish. For easier digestion and better absorption, grind flaxseeds before use (then keep in the refrigerator and use within a week). The oil is very temperature sensitive and quickly becomes rancid if left open to the air; keep in the refrigerator once opened. The are also known as linseed.

GOJI BERRIES

These shriveled, reddish orange berries first found use in Chinese medicine can now be found easily in all health food stores and some grocery stores and supermarkets. They have a slightly sweet but herbal taste. Sprinkle them over breakfast, into muffin batters, yogurt, or granola, or plump them up in hot water to use in salads for an antioxidant boost to the day.

GLUTEN-FREE FLOUR MIX

An already made mix of nonwheat flours (usually rice, potato, buckwheat flours, and cornstarch/cornflour), this is a very useful substitute for all-purpose (plain) flour and, if you add baking powder, self-rising (self-raising) flour. This is very helpful for people with gluten intolerance. More and more people have problems with gluten but love to eat "normal" bread. Some gluten-free flour mixes are highly refined, but there are brands that use brown rice, buckwheat, chia seeds, and healthier ingredients than the older brands.

HARISSA PASTE

This rich spicy paste made from dried red chiles, oil, garlic, coriander, and other spices is widely used in North African cooking. A little goes a long way. Use harissa as a rub or marinade for vegetables and beans, or swirl into dips and dressings for a hit of heat.

HEMP SEEDS

Not to be confused with its mind-altering cousin, edible hemp seeds are very high in essential fatty acids and contain all the essential amino acids humans need. This makes them ideal for a meat-free diet. Shell-on seeds are very crunchy and can be hard to chew, which is why in some recipes I process them first. Shelled hemp seeds (sometimes called hemp hearts) are softer but have shorter shelf life and offer much less fiber. Hemp seeds are crushed to make hemp seed oil.

INCAN GOLDEN BERRIES

These cherry-size, heavily seeded yellow fruits grow hidden within a papery calyx that looks like a lantern. You may already know them as Cape gooseberries or physalis. With a sweet sour flavor, fresh Incan golden berries add color and zing to salads and salsas. They are available dried, too.

JULIENNE VEGETABLE PEELER

This handy tool peels vegetables and firm fruit into thin, straight strips about ⅛ inch (3 mm) across, and is so much faster than chopping by hand. Use to make vegetable "spaghetti" or "noodles," If you already have a spiralizer (see Spiralizer, page 234), you can use that instead.

KELP NOODLES

A gluten- and grain-free alternative to the norm, these translucent noodles are made from seaweed, which is rich in minerals. Much like "glass" or rice noodles, kelp noodles take on the flavor of whatever they are cooked in. Some brands are ready to eat from the package after a quick rinse, while some require precooking or soaking before you enjoy them in soups and salads.

LUCUMA POWDER

This natural sweetener was another favorite of the Incas, now finding fame as a superfood. It is made from drying and then grinding the golden flesh from lucuma fruit, which grows across South America. I use the powder as a sweetening ingredient, the flavor being slightly maple-syrup-ish and malty and particularly good with chocolate.

MACA POWDER

Another favorite ingredient from the mountains of Peru, maca powder is made from the maca root, which is from the radish family. Known for its energy-boosting properties, maca is thought to improve immunity, red blood cell production, and sexual desire. Maca can alter hormonal balance, so check with a health-care provider if you have any conditions that may be affected.

MATCHA POWDER

This is Japanese high-grade green tea, powdered very finely. Now a globally popular ingredient, it is baked into cakes, swirled into lattes, and revered as a flavoring in its own right. As with other types of tea, matcha is popular for its detoxifying powers, but remember it is high in caffeine, and gives quite a buzz.

MESQUITE

Mesquite powder is made from the fruiting pod of the leguminous mesquite tree (yes, the one that lends a sweet smokiness to barbecue food). It is a high-protein ingredient that is sweet, yet also low GI with a rich, nutty caramel flavor. It thickens and enriches drinks and smoothies, in particular and can also be used as a flour replacer.

MILLET AND MILLET FLAKES

I like to use these small, round seeds as an alternative to rice or couscous, or in their flaked (crushed) form to make oatmeal (porridge). The flavor is fairly plain, and best enhanced with a light toasting before the seeds are soaked or used for baking. Millet was one of the first crops to be cultivated, and remains an important global staple food.

MINI GRINDER
A small grinder, sold specifically for grinding coffee beans or spices, will break down very hard whole spices and grains quickly and easily.

MORINGA POWDER
Made from the ground leaves of the Moringa tree, this supplement is very high in protein, a natural multivitamin, and contains plenty of iron, too. You can add it to smoothies, dressings, and even pestos.

MULBERRIES
There are many different varieties of mulberry, grown wild or cultivated across the continents, from North America to the Indian subcontinent. Shaped like an elongated blackberry and either red, white, or black, they make sweet pickings for fall (autumn) foragers and are delicious in preserves, baked goods, and desserts. If you can't find mulberries, use blackberries instead.

NUT BUTTER
Whole roasted nuts are processed to a smooth or slightly chunky paste that is high in protein, unsaturated fats, antioxidants, vitamins, and minerals. See Almond Butter, page 229.

NUT MILK BAG
This is a finely woven fabric bag designed to filter liquid away from the nut pulp after making homemade nut milk; however, I use one for straining juices and squeezing out liquid from vegetables, too. You can use a cheesecloth (muslin cloth) or a jelly bag, or a large square of any fine, white, clean fabric instead, if needed. Just spread the fabric over a bowl and add whatever it is you need to drain. Bunch the fabric up into a bag and tie securely. Either hang the bag, squeeze with your hands, or let it drain in a strainer over a large bowl.

NUTRITIONAL YEAST FLAKES
Made from a yeast that is cultured on sugar cane then washed and dried, these yellow flakes have a strong *umami* flavor that is similar to Parmesan cheese, and are used widely in vegan cooking to give a cheesy or eggy flavor. The flakes are high in B vitamins, folic acid, and other good nutrients and can be sprinkled onto food as it is, or used in sauces, dressings, savory casseroles, "cheese" spreads, and more. Nutritional yeast is inactive so won't cause food to froth, ferment, or rise.

OAT MILK
Dried oats are soaked in water, then drained, rinsed, then blended with water, strained, and then sweetened to taste. A dairy-free alternative to milk with a neutral flavor, oat milk is useful for smoothies, oatmeals (porridges), and baking. It can be a little on the thin side, so if you prefer a thicker milk look for a recipe that uses a few cashew nuts, too.

ONION POWDER
This is simply dehydrated and then granulated onion. It has a strong savory flavor that adds depth to burger mixes, dressings, and dips, or is good for sprinkling onto snacks. You can make your own if you have a dehydrator.

PHYTONUTRIENTS
Beneficial nutritional compounds found within plant foods, *phyto* coming from the word for "plant" in ancient Greek. You will have heard of many of these before, for example, carotenoids from orange foods. Phytonutrients aren't essential for life, but help keep your body running along more happily and may prevent ailments and diseases.

PROBIOTIC POWDER
Probiotics provide a healthy dose of live, good bacteria, which can help balance the digestive system and treat related problems. The better your gut flora, the better you feel. I use powdered probiotics in recipes that would usually use dairy, and include active *Lactobacillus acidophilus* and *Bifidobacteria*. If you use this in a cheesecake, it will heighten the tangy/cheese flavor.

PSYLLIUM HUSK
Gluten-free flours cannot offer the same stretch and chew that wheat flours provide to baked goods, but psyllium husk can improve things. Because it sits with the liquid in the mixed dough, psyllium becomes gummy and elastic. In breads leavened with baking soda (bicarbonate of soda) or yeast, this stretches as your bread bakes, in turn trapping the bubbles of carbon dioxide (CO_2) and helping your bread to rise. You will often find this in the health section of your local store, sold as a high fiber supplement.

QUINOA

This versatile Andean staple contains all nine essential amino acids, which make it a complete protein. It is also very high in anti-inflammatory phytonutrients, vitamins, minerals, and fiber. Simmer or soak it until tender and a small "tail" (the germ) pops out from the main part of the grain. Both red and white varieties are slightly bitter and nutty in flavor and require thorough washing before use. Quinoa is gluten free.

RAS-EL-HANOUT

A classic Moroccan spice mixture, ras el hanout contains many aromatic spices, including cinnamon, cumin, coriander, cloves, pepper, ginger, and even edible dried rose petals. If you can't find it, simply use a combination of these spices instead.

RAW CACAO NIBS

These are the chocolaty heart of the cocoa bean. Once cocoa beans are fermented, dried, and roasted, the shells are removed and the nibs are exposed. Very crunchy and with a bitter chocolate flavor, I add nibs to give texture and flavor to raw baked goods. They can be finely chopped, crushed, or even ground to a powder and used in hot drinks, giving a rich cocoa flavor to vegan recipes where regular chocolate would be a no-no.

RAW CACAO POWDER

Raw cacao comes from raw cacao pods that have been sundried rather than roasted, then cold-pressed to separate the cacao fat from the cacao. This gentle approach means that the cacao powder retains more of its natural phytonutrients and enzymes than cocoa powder, which is made from roasted cacao. Raw cacao powder has a very strong chocolate flavor.

RAW CHOCOLATE

This is made by blending raw cacao powder and raw cacao butter, then sweetening it. Raw bars will usually be sweetened with coconut sugar or lucuma powder and flavored with a little vanilla.

REISHI MUSHROOM POWDER

Another staple of Chinese medicine, deep red reishi mushrooms are said to be anti-inflammatory and contain high levels of antioxidants to promote better well-being and long life. They are most palatable in powdered form, which is easily added to drinks and smoothies. Seek advice before using reishi mushroom powder if you take blood pressure or blood-clotting medications.

REJUVELAC

Leave sprouted grains in fresh water at the right temperature and they will begin to ferment—in a good way. Friendly bacteria start to produce acids, which in turn prevent harmful bacteria from growing. The resulting liquid—rejuvelac—is then taken as a natural probiotic drink to help improve digestive health.

SAMBAL OELEK

A very spicy uncooked chili sauce used in Indonesian cuisine. It has a slightly chunky texture, with clearly visible chile seeds and often includes salt and lime or lemon juice. *Sambal* means "sauce," and *oelek* refers to the mortar and pestle traditionally used to pound the ingredients together. Use it wherever you want to add plenty of heat, or instead of fresh chile.

SHATAVARIA

This root extract, popular in Ayurvedic medicine, is said to be particularly beneficial for women, promoting hormonal balance with naturally occurring plant-based estrogens. Ashwagandha is the equivalent Indian "ginseng" for men.

SKYR

Skyr is a traditional cultured milk enjoyed in Iceland. It is a very thick yogurt. The milk, usually using sheep or cow milk, is curdled using bacterial cultures and often rennet. The curds are strained to become thick skyr.

SPELT FLOUR

Called the "marching grain" by the Romans for its energy content, spelt fell by the wayside as wheat became easier to grow. Spelt is a member of the wheat family—so it isn't strictly suitable for people with severe wheat intolerance or allergies but can be, for some, easier to digest than wheat gluten. A hybrid of an ancient wheat grain and grass, spelt has a complex, slightly sour, ryelike flavor. I like to use it for pizza crusts (bases).

SPIRALIZER

A kitchen gadget that quickly turns vegetables into long spiral-like strings by rotating them against a small, sharp blade. A julienne peeler is a more economical option, although it will cut your vegetables a little finer.

SOAKING NUTS

Soaking nuts overnight in salted water before use is also known as activating. This process stimulates germination in the nut, which increases its nutritional value, just as sprouting does for seeds and grains. Soaking also reduces the amount of a substance called phytic acid in the raw nut, which inhibits mineral absorption.

SOURDOUGH STARTER

To start your own starter from scratch will take about a week. Start by stirring together equal amounts of water and spelt flour in a jar, lightly cover, and keep in a warm place for 12 hours. Then feed twice a day (every 12 hours) as instructed on page 118 with scant ½ cup (3½ fl oz/100 ml) water and ½ cup (2¼ oz/60 g) flour. On day 3 discard half the starter and then feed as usual. Repeat every 12 hours. When your starter becomes bubbly and starts to grow noticeably after feeds it is ready to use. This will be on day 5–7, depending on the temperature and the quality of flour.

SPROUTER

If you get really into sprouting your own seeds and grains, then it could be worth buying a sprouter, which is essentially a stacking system of trays. The trays are perforated to allow air to circulate between the layers of sprouting seeds, preventing mold or getting the sprouts too wet.

STEVIA

Stevia is a sweetener, extracted from the stevia leaf. Although it is still a highly processed product, it does come from a natural source. Stevia is many times sweeter than sugar and can be either granulated or in liquid form—and even in flavored drops.

SUPERFOOD

There's no strict definition of what a superfood is, but we're in no doubt that some foods, such as garlic, blueberries, and quinoa are "super," because they either have superior levels of antioxidants, phytonutrients, and healthy fats (or more than one of the above) that support the immune system and promote health. A superfood, however, is not a silver bullet.

The important thing is to enjoy a wide range of fruit and vegetables in a healthy, balanced diet.

TAMARI

An almost always gluten-free soy sauce from Japan (check the label as brands do vary), tamari has a slightly richer, sweeter flavor than regular soy sauce and is a little less salty and more balanced. It is traditionally a by-product of miso paste production.

TAMARIND PASTE

Tamarind paste has an unusual sourness that adds a tart background flavor to many Asian, Indian, and Mexican recipes. The paste is made from the sticky pulp within the ripe, brown tamarind pods, which look like long brown beans, dangling from the tamarind tree as they ripen in the tropical heat. Buy it in a jar or tub and keep in the refrigerator once opened. Tamarind has a cleansing effect on the digestion.

VANILLA POWDER

Vanilla beans (pods) are dried at a low temperature, then finely ground. I use this delicious powder instead of more processed liquid vanilla extract, adding natural sweetness and a strong vanilla flavor to breakfast recipes, desserts, and drinks.

VEGETABLE BOUILLON

This is vegetable stock powder that can be spooned straight into recipes or made up to a liquid broth (stock) using boiling water. A good brand will add plenty of base flavor of its own and also enhance the other ingredients in your recipe.

WHEATGRASS POWDER

Wheatgrass is simply the very young green shoots from the wheat plant. Becasue wheatgrass leaves and juice do not contain any part of the grain, they are gluten free. The leaves contain high levels of chlorophyll, antioxidants, vitamins and minerals, which are dried then ground to a powder. They are an easy win for morning smoothies and shakes.

ZA'ATAR

A tasty blend of sumac, dried thyme, sesame seeds, and salt, za'atar is used to flavor and finish many Middle Eastern recipes. Some blends include cumin and dried oregano too. It has a sourish, savory flavor (that's due to the sumac, a tangy, lemony spice).

Recipe Notes

Unless otherwise stated, individual vegetables and fruits, such as onions and apples, are assumed to be medium.

All herbs are fresh, unless otherwise specified.

Cooking and dehydrating times are for guidance only, as individual ovens and dehydrators vary. If using a convection (fan) oven, follow the manufacturer's instructions concerning oven temperatures.

Exercise a high level of caution when following recipes involving any potentially hazardous activity, including the use of high temperatures and open flames.

Make an appointment to see your doctor before starting a new diet plan, especially if you have underlying medical conditions or are pregnant.

Some nut-free recipes include coconut, coconut products, and/or pine nuts. The coconut is classified as a dry drupe, while the brown, fibrous coconut is its seed. Pine nuts, meanwhile, are actually seeds, and so may be safe for some people with a tree nut allergy to eat. Some individuals are allergic to these foods without being allergic to tree nuts; people with nut allergies may also suffer from additional allergies to coconuts or pine nuts. If you have a tree nut allergy, it is best to exercise caution with these foods and consult your doctor.

Some recipes include bee pollen. These should be avoided by pregnant and breastfeeding women, and anyone who has experienced pollen allergies.

Some recipes include raw or very lightly cooked eggs and fermented products. These should be avoided by the elderly, infants, pregnant women, convalescents, and anyone with an impaired immune system.

Exercise caution when making fermented products, ensuring all equipment is spotlessly clean, and seek expert advice if in any doubt.

When no quantity is specified, for example of oils, salts, and herbs used for finishing dishes, quantities are discretionary and flexible.

All herbs, shoots, flowers, berries, and leaves should be picked fresh from a clean source. Exercise caution when foraging for ingredients; any foraged ingredients should only be eaten if an expert has deemed them safe to eat.

Both metric and imperial measures are used in this book. Follow one set of measurements throughout, not a mixture, as they are not interchangeable.

All spoon and cup measurements are level, unless otherwise stated. 1 teaspoon = 5 ml; 1 tablespoon = 15 ml. Australian standard tablespoons are 20 ml, so Australian readers are advised to use 3 teaspoons in place of 1 tablespoon when measuring small quantities.

Index

Page numbers in italics refer to photographs.

SOLLA EIRÍKSDÓTTIR is well known in Iceland as a vegetarian and a passionate advocate of organic foods. She started her first vegetarian restaurant twenty years ago and today she runs five successful restaurants, an organic market, and has her own organic food brand, Himneskt, sold in grocery stores and supermarkets across Iceland. Solla has published five cookbooks, co-authored a few more, written articles on organic food, and taught vegetarian cooking on television as well as regularly teaching seminars on raw food. She is an enthusiastic proponent of an organic and sustainable lifestyle, and has helped to make both vegetarianism and organic foods more mainstream and widely available in Iceland. Solla has twice been elected "best RAW gourmet chef" and "best RAW simple chef" in the International Best of Raw contest. She is a vibrant speaker and gives demonstrations every year at The Longevity Now conference in LA.

HILDUR ÁRSÆLSDÓTTIR is Solla's eldest daughter. Hildur is a violinist and also plays the musical saw, like her great grandfather. Through music she has traveled the world with her band, Amiina. She inherited her family's enthusiasm for living a healthy, organic vegetarian lifestyle and in 2013 Hildur finished a BSc degree in nutritional science from the University of Iceland. She hopes to pursue further studies in the field of nutrition in the future.

Solla and Hildur love to spend time together in their kitchen and vegetable garden. They also share an interest in protecting the environment and inspire each other to try out new ways of leading a more eco-friendly lifestyle.

Phaidon Press Limited
Regent's Wharf
All Saints Street
London N1 9PA

Phaidon Press Inc.
65 Bleecker Street
New York, NY 10012
phaidon.com

First published 2016
© 2016 Phaidon Press Limited
ISBN 978 0 7148 7114 1

A CIP catalogue record for this book is available from the British Library and the Library of Congress.

Commissioning Editor: Ellie Smith
Project Editor: Sophie Hodgkin
Production Controller: Leonie Kellman

Designed by Studio Otamendi
Photography by Simon Bajada

The publisher would like to thank Theresa Bebbington, Jane Hornby, Isobel McLean, Kathy Steer, and Lauren Utvich for their contributions to the book.

Printed in China